# OLD SHIRBURNIAN NAVY & ARMY LIST,

## 1914–1919.

SHERBORNE:
F. BENNETT AND CO., LTD., PRINTERS
MCMXXI.

# PREFACE

## TO THE

## THIRD AND FINAL EDITION.

IT is more than five years since the Second Edition of this Roll of Service and Honour was issued, and more than three since the Armistice, which was the beginning of the end of the War,—that end which even now is not fulfilled. Such blame as is due for this delay I must take to myself: with greater energy and method I should have completed the work long ago, or, better still, have caused it to be completed. I believe, however, that my brother Shirburnians will with their usual kindness be to my faults a little blind, especially when they consider the perplexities of these years and the multiplicity of duties laid upon me by the vigorous development of the School. The difficulty of collecting the mass of facts which are here represented in a much abbreviated form can only be appreciated by those who have undertaken similar compilations. Very little of the actual labour has been mine. The first stage of preparing the original

*Corpus* of this Edition was kindly undertaken by Mr. Walter Lloyd, O.S., who made a card index of all the names and relevant facts that he could collect. The later stages of editing and augmenting this material owe most, once more, to the devoted energy of Mr. P. A. Baker, my former Secretary, who was himself dangerously wounded in France in 1917. Among many other helpers, the chief thanks are due to Major Davis and Captain Bensly, D.S.O., and to Sergeant-Major Wood, particularly in regard to the Distinctions. My present Secretary, Mr. E. A. Gibbs, has also given me indispensable assistance. To all these, and to others too numerous to mention, I desire to express sincere gratitude, not only on my own behalf but still more on behalf of our Shirburnian brotherhood, which, as the fruit of their labours, possesses a record of inexhaustible interest to us all and, as we hope, of perennial inspiration to succeeding generations of Shirburnians.

It is inevitable that there should be some mistakes and omissions in such a list. For any that were avoidable I ask pardon, only pleading that very great pains have been taken to make the list as correct and complete as possible. It is practically certain that no further edition will be printed: the cost of the present one far exceeds any sum that will be realised from the sale of copies. But any corrections will be thankfully received, if addressed to

O.S. RECORDS,
SCHOOL HOUSE,
SHERBORNE, DORSET,

and will be noted in a special copy kept in the School Library.

NOWELL SMITH,
Headmaster.

December, 1921.

## HOUSES.

School House *(a)*.

James', Curteis', Wood's, Whitehead's, Wildman's, Carey's *(b)*.

Tancock's, Wilson's, Dunkin's *(c)*.

Blanch's, Bell's, Bensly's, Tindall's *(d)*.

Hetherington's, Rhoades', Hodgson's, King's *(f)*.

Milford's, Ross's *(g)*.

Town *(T)*.

Preparatory *(Prep.)*.

## SIGNS.

†=killed. The Roll of Honour is printed on pages 149, 150, 151, 152, 153, 154, 155.

*=decorated or mentioned in despatches. It is not necessary to print a separate list of these distinctions.

# ADDENDA AND CORRIGENDA.

The following information was received too late for inclusion in the main list.

†Abbot, Lieut. E. J. W.—read, Abbott.

Abbot, Lieut. F. G. W.—read, Abbott; house *c*.

*Adams, Lieut.-Com. (Bt.Com.) B. F.—read, mentioned in despatches (twice); D.S.O.

*Anstruther, Capt. (a./Lieut.-Col.) P. N.—add, mentioned in despatches (twice).

*Applin, Major and Bt. Lieut.-Col. R.V.K.—add, mentioned for war services.

*Baird, Major R. E.—add, O.B.E.

Baker, 2nd Lieut. A. M. S. ... 1913-17 *f*
Royal Garrison Artillery.

*Ball, Capt. E. P.—add, O.B.E.

*Barker, Capt. R. E.—Kurdistan, 1918-20, not 1918-19.

Bartlett, Lieut. H. G.—read, Bartleet.

Bevan, Sub-Lieut. B. B. ... 1910-11 *a*
R.N.R.

Beven, L.-Corpl. A. L. H. ... 1912-13 *g*
Tank Corps.

Blakeley, Lieut. H. P.—read, Blakely.

*Birks, a./Capt. (temp. Major) E. R.—read, mentioned in despatches (twice).

Bond, Lieut. Denys ... ... 1894-98 *a*
At Dartmouth till August, 1917; then served in Intelligence Division of the Admiralty War Staff with a Commission as Lieut. R.N.V.R. until end of war.

Bradford, W. G. ... ... 1902-9 *a*
No definite information, but believed Capt. in Somerset Light Infantry.

*Campbell-Orde, Lieut. A. C. ... 1912-15 *a*
Mentioned for war services; A.F.C.

*Collins, Major C. H. G. ... ... 1900 *T.*
D.C.L.I.; Staff Capt., Alexandria, 1915; A.A.Q.M.G., 53rd Welsh Division, 1917; D.A.A.G., Northern Division, Army of the Rhine, 1919; O.B.E.

Corke, Lieut. T. D. ... ... 1907-9 *b*
R.M.C., Sandhurst, 1916; Lieut., Middlesex Regiment, 1919.

*Deacon, Bt. Lieut.-Col. H. R. G.—read, mentions in despatches (four times).

de Pass, G.—correct initials G. V. A.

Dow, Sergt. W. I.—correct initials W. J.

*Farrer, Major E. R. B.—read, mentioned in despatches (thrice); O.B.E.

*Flack, 2nd Lieut. H. L.—correct rank Major.

Flower, Lieut. E. J.—correct dates, 1911-14 *a*.

Flower, 2nd Lieut. W. M.—correct dates, 1913-16 *g*.

†Fraser, 2nd Lieut. V. A. D.—correct initials O.A.D.

*Freeman, Major C. T.—D.S.C. not D.S.O.

†Foley, Pte. E. B. ... ... 1905 *a*
Pte. in Canadian Forces; served in France; wounded, and prisoner in Germany for two years; died from effects of wounds, 1921.

Frisby, C. G. ... ... ... 1908-11 *b*
Joined up in East Africa; invalided out; (rank and unit not known).

Garland, 2nd Lieut. E. A. ... 1912-16 *c*
Worcestershire Regiment.

*Gibbons, 2nd Lieut. H.—add, M.C.

GILL, Major E. E. ... ... 1902-6 *a*

†GRIERSON, Lieut. S.D.—correct initials S.V.

*HOBSON, Capt. E. R. C.—add, D.F.C.

HOPKINS, J. G. H. ... ... 1905-8 *b*
2nd Rhodesian Regiment (rank not known).

*IREMONGER, Col. E. A.—C.B.E. not G.B.E.

*KEIR, Surgeon Comdr. W. W.—read, mentioned in despatches (thrice).

*LAMB, Major D. G.—add, mentioned for war services.

LEE, 2nd Lieut. C. J.—correct initials C. I.

†*LIMBERY, Capt. C. R.—read, mentioned in despatches (twice).

†*LIMBERY, Capt. K. T.—read, mentioned in despatches (twice).

*LUCAS, Lieut. D.—should be starred.

LUXTON, Gentleman Cadet A. R. 1914-18 *f*
R.M.C., Sandhurst, 1918.

MAYBURY, Cadet M.—correct initials L. M.

MILLAR, Lieut. J. G. ... 1906-11 *T.* attached *b*
Indian Army, 1/19th Punjabis, 1918.

*MOBERLEY, Bt. Lt.-Col. A. H.—read, MOBERLY.

MONCKTON, Lieut. J. P.—correct initials I. P.

*MOORE, Major C. G. H.—should be starred.

NICHOLS, 2nd Lieut. W. N.—read, NICHOLLS; house *c* not *g*.

NORSWORTHY, Lieut. E. ... 1905-8 *f*
R.A.S.C.; served in France.

†PEARSON, Cadet C. R. ... ... 1901-3 *b*
Cadet in Merchant Service; accidentally killed on H.M.S. Thistle, December, 1914.

PETERSON, Midshipman G. F. ... 1913-17 *f*
R.N.C., Keyham; Midshipman, June, 1918, H.M.S. Revenge.

PIM, Flight Cadet I.M.—correct initials J.M.

POWELL, Rev. J. R.—read, Army Chaplains' Department; attached 2/17th London Regiment, 60th Division Artillery; and Staffordshire Yeomanry in Palestine, 1917 to 1919.

*RICKETT, Major G. R.—read, Lieut.-Col.; R.A.M.C. (T.); R.M.O., Dorset Yeomanry, 1914 to 1915; O.C. No. 88 General Hospital, E.E.F., Cairo, 1915 to 1919; mentioned in despatches (thrice); O.B.E.

*SLOMAN, Brig.-Genl. H. S., D.S.O.—read, mentioned in despatches; twice mentioned for war services.

SMITH, Lieut. D. F. ... ... 1906-8 *b*
Royal Fusiliers, 22nd Bn.

STREATFIELD, 2nd Lieut. T. B. M.—read, STREATFEILD.

†STUART-FRENCH (STUART), Major C. H. ... ... ... 1881-2 *f*
Inniskilling Fusiliers; D.A.Q.M.G. to Gen. Burn Murdock; died on active service, December 23rd, 1916, of heart failure.

STUART-FRENCH (STUART), Major Pascoe W. G., J.P. ... ... ... 1881-4 *f*
1914, Supt. of Cork Remount Depôt; 1915, Capt.; 1917 to 1919, in France, as Major, with Remounts.

TULLIS, Capt. G. D. E., M.B. ... 1905-7 *c*
R.A.M.C.; temp. Lieut., December, 1915; Capt., 1916; served with 23rd Division and 50th Casualty Clearing Station in France and Flanders; demobilised, December, 1918.

*TURTON, Major M. S.—read, mentioned in despatches (thrice).

WALSH, Col. H. A., C.B.—starred by mistake.

*WILSON, Capt. R. H.—add, M.C.

# OLD SHIRBURNIAN NAVY & ARMY LIST

(ARRANGED ALPHABETICALLY).

*ABELL, Major C. F. ... ... 1902-4 *f*

R.N.V.R.(H.M. Air Service); Lieutenant, R.N.V.R., attached R.N.A.S., May, 1915; promoted Lieut.-Comdr., R. N. V. R., December, 1917; transferred as Major R.A.F., April, 1918; Military O.B.E.

*ABELL, Major G. H. ... ... 1900-3 *f*

R.N.V.R.; Lieutenant for engineering duties R.N.A.S., August, 1915; promoted Lieut.-Comdr., January, 1917; transferred to R.A.F. as Major (Technical), April, 1918; mentioned in despatches; O.B.E.

†ABBOT, Lieut. E. J. W. ... 1898-1903 *c*

The Royal Inniskilling Fusiliers, 2nd Bn., attached 4th Bn. (extra Reserve), and then to Royal Irish Fusiliers; killed at Festubert (or Richebourg), May 16th or 17th, 1915.

ABBOT, Lieut. F. G. W. ... 1903-4

Prince Albert's (Somerset Light Infantry), 8th Bn.; attached 9th (Reserve) Bn.; transferred to 6th (S.) Bn., B.E.F., France.

ADAMS, Sub-Lieut. N. ... ... 1908-12 *Prep.*

R.N.; H.M.S. Courageous.

ADAMS, Lieut. A. G. ... ... 1906-13 *T.&g*

I.A.R.O.; on duty with the Burma Military Police in connection with the Kuki Punitive Measures Force, Chin Hills, Burma.

*ADAMS, Lieut.-Com. (Bt.Com.) B.F. 1900-2 *c*

H.M.S. Cumberland; mentioned in despatches.

*ADAMS, Capt. G. H. ... ... 1901-4 *c*

Australian Field Artillery, 48th Batt.; M.C.

ADAMS, Sub-Lieut. H. ... ... 1906-11 *Prep.*

R.N.; Served 1914, H.M.S. Emperor of India; 1916, H.M.S. Agincourt; 1918, was present in destroyer in attacks on Zeebrugge and Ostend.

ADAMS, Capt. H. R. ... ... 1906-10 *T.*

Honourable Artillery Company; served April, 1915, with 1st (Infantry) Bn., Machine Gun Section (wounded at Hooge, June, 1915); and with 3rd (Infantry) Bn. in France from December, 1916, to December, 1917; Adjutant of 2/72nd Punjabis, Indian Army, February, 1918.

ADAMS, Lieut. O. P. ... ... 1908-13 *T.&g*

R.F.A., 3/75th Brigade; served in France; and in Mesopotamia with 1/4th Bn. (T.), the Dorsetshire Regiment.

ADAMS, temp./Lieut.-Col. R. J. ... 1893-8 *T.*

Indian Army, Commanding 20th Bn., 131st United Provinces Regiment, previously in Indian Police.

†ADAMSON, Capt. W. ... 1899-1903 *a*
The Loyal North Lancashire Regiment, 11th (Reserve) Bn.; killed in Mesopotamia, April 23rd or 24th, 1916.

ADAMTHWAITE, 2nd Lieut. J. W. E. 1906-9 *c*
Royal Army Service Corps, 2nd Notts and Derby Mounted Brigade.

ADDINGTON, Major W. L. ... 1868-71 *b*
The Queen's (Royal West Surrey) Regiment (Ret. pay); employed at Depôt, 'The Queen's' Regiment, September, 1914, to January, 1918.

ADDISON, J. F. P. ... ... 1903-4 *b*
Cyclist Corps and R.N. Division (Anson Bn.); served in France; wounded.

ADYE, Capt. L. C. ... ... 1907-11 *c*
The Duke of Wellington's (West Riding Regiment), 3rd Bn. (Reserve); attached 2nd Bn.; gas poisoned May 5th, 1915; wounded July 1st, 1916; non-combatant from May 5th, 1917.

AGAR, Pte. B. M. S. ... ... 1909-13 *b*
The Royal Fusiliers (City of London Regiment), Public Schools Bn.

AINSLIE, Sub-Lieut. W. St. J. ... 1909-12 *Prep.*
R.N.; Served on H.M.S. Queen Elizabeth from May, 1917, to Armistice.

†ALDERSON, Capt. A. G. J. ... 1914-16 *Master*
The Duke of Cornwall's Light Infantry, 2/5th Bn. (T.); Lieutenant, Machine Gun Corps; killed in accident during bombing practice at Grantham, October 19th, 1916.

ALEXANDER, Lieut. K. E. ... 1911-16 *g*

The Durham Light Infantry, 2nd Bn.; served in France; severely wounded and taken prisoner March 21st, 1918; reached home January 4th, 1919; demobilized, April 17th, 1919; Special Reserve of Officers.

ANDERSON, Col. R. F. H. ... 1872-7 *a*

(Indian Army, Retired) Assistant Provost Marshal, Q.M.G., 17th Division.

ANDERSON, Lieut. W. H. ... 1902-3 *b*

The Gloucestershire Regiment, 1/6th Bn. (T.).

ANSON, 2nd Lieut. C. O. ... 1914-17 *a*

Royal Air Force, R.A.F. Station, Fowlmere, Royston, Herts.

*ANSTRUTHER, Capt. (a./Lieut.-Col.) P. N. ... ... ... 1905-9 *d*

The Queen's Own (Royal West Kent) Regiment, 2nd Bn.; Adjt. 7th (S.) Bn.; D.S.O., M.C.

*APLIN, Bt. Col. P. J. H. ... 1873-6 *a*

Indian Army, 1st Class Interpreter; Commanding 18th (S.) Bn. (1st Public Works, Pioneers), The Duke of Cambridge's Own (Middlesex Regiment); D.S.O.

*APPLIN, Major and Bt. Lieut.-Col. R. V. K. ... ... ... 1883-6 *a*

14th Hussars; Instructor, Machine Gun Corps Training Centre, July, 1916, to October, 1917; mentioned in despatches; D.S.O.

†Armstrong, Lieut.-Col. C. A. ... 1888-9 *f*

The Northumberland Fusiliers; 2nd in Command, 8th (S.) Bn.; killed in France, October 1st, 1915.

†Awdry, Lieut. W. W. ... ... 1911-14 *d*

The Duke of Edinburgh's (Wiltshire Regiment); died, April 14th, 1918, of wounds received same day near Kemmell Hill.

†Bacchus, Capt. and Adjt. W. H. O. 1901-2 *a*

The York and Lancaster Regiment, 1st Bn.; died September 13th, 1915, of wounds received in Flanders.

*Back, Capt. G. A., M.B. (Camb.) 1906-10 *a*

R.A.M.C.; served in France, Mesopotamia and Persia; mentioned in despatches.

*Baddeley, Capt. S. E. L. ... 1900-4 *a*

19th Lancers (Fane's House), Indian Army; served in France with the Indian Contingents; from February, 1918, with the Egyptian Expeditionary Force; mentioned in despatches.

Bailey, Capt. C. H. ... ... 1910-12 *d*

The Monmouthshire Regiment, 1st Bn.; resigned through ill-health, March, 1916.

Baird, Major R. E. ... ... 1892-7 *a*

The Highland Light Infantry; attached 1st Garrison Bn., Royal Scots Fusiliers.

†Baker, Capt. C. D. ... ... 1886-9 *Price*

Grenadier Guards (Special Reserve); attached 1st Bn.; killed in France, July 29th, 1917.

*Baker, Lieut.-Col. E. E. F. ... 1908-14 *f*
The Duke of Cambridge's Own (Middlesex Regiment), 5th Bn., attached 2nd Bn.; mentioned in despatches (twice); M.C. with bar; D.S.O.

†Baker, 2nd Lieut. G. L. J. ... 1910-15 *f*
Middlesex Regiment; killed in action, 28th April, 1917.

*Bakewell, Lieut. (a./Major) W. B. 1908-13 *f*
The Queen's Own (Royal West Kent Regiment), 5th Bn. (T.); seconded, Machine Gun Corps, 286th Coy., Abbottabad, N.W.F.P., India; mentioned in despatches.

Ball, Capt. E. P. ... 1905-1905 *d*
110th Mahratta Light Infantry.

†Bamford, Pte. A. ... ... 1903-5 *f*
Grenadier Guards; killed, near Loos, October 11th, 1915.

*Bamford, Bt. Major E. ... ... 1900-2 *T.*
Royal Marine Light Infantry, H.M.S. Royal Sovereign; mentioned in despatches; V.C., D.S.O.; Order of St. Anne, 3rd Class (Russian); Légion d'Honneur.

Bamford, Lieut. R. ... ... 1897-1900 *T.*
Royal Army Service Corps, Mechanical Transport; served one year as private in The London Regiment, 25th (County of London) Cyclist Bn.; in France from November, 1915.

Barclay, Sergt. W. E. A. ... 1901-6 *b*
Canadian Gordon Highlanders.

BARCLAY, Paymaster-Lieut. J. C. H. 1907-10 *b*
H.M.S. Hercules.

*BARDSWELL, Major N. D., M.D., F.R.C.P., F.R.S. (Edin.) ... ... 1886-9 *c*
R.A.M.C. Service:—Netley Hospital; Mediterranean E.F. (O.C. Malta R.A.M.C. detachment for duty in Sicily, 1915); Hospital Ship 'Britannic'; B.E.F., France; M.V.O.

*BARKER, Capt. R. E. ... ... 1904-7 *d*
The Prince of Wales's Volunteers (South Lancashire Regiment), 1st Bn.; attached 33rd Signal Company, Mesopotamia E.F., 1916-18; mentioned in despatches (thrice); special employ, Kurdistan, Persia, 1918; Political, Kurdistan, 1918-19.

†BARNES, 2nd Lieut. (a./Capt.) J.E.T. 1907-13 *f*
The Gloucester Regiment, 7th (S.) Bn.; served in Gallipoli (August, 1915), in Egypt, and in the attempted relief of Kut; killed, 3rd February, 1917, in Mesopotamia.

BARNES, Major S. F. ... ... 1903-7 *a*
Territorial Force Reserve; Royal Garrison Artillery, 3rd (Portland) Company, Dorsetshire R.G.A.; coast defence, Portland, August, 1914, to March, 1916; then, B.E.F., France, with 123rd Siege Battery, R.G.A., to April, 1917; 502nd Siege Battery, R.G.A., September, 1917, to February, 1918; then posted to No. 2 S.A.R.B.; G.S., November, 1918.

†BARRY, Capt. N. J. M. ... 1898-1900 *c*
East African Transport Corps; killed in German East Africa, October 21st, 1917.

Barter, Lieut. C. M. ... ... 1912-16 *g*

Royal Air Force; 44th, 49th and 51st Foreign Squadrons.

Bartlett, Lieut. H. G. ... 1906-9 *c*

The Essex Regiment, 3rd Bn. (Special Reserve); attached 1st Bn.; acting Adjt. on Peninsular from October to December, 1915; wounded at Beaumont Hamel, August, 1916; invalided out, January, 1918.

Bartlett, Corpl. E. P. ... 1910-12 *d*

The Dorsetshire Regiment, 2/4th Bn. (T.).

*Barton, Capt. H. G. M. ... 1897-9 *d*

Royal Engineers; mentioned in despatches.

Basevi, Lieut.-Col. W. H. ... 1877-80 *a*

Army Pay Department; Staff Paymaster, Base VI.

Bashall, Corpl. W. H. ... ... 1901-5 *a*

83rd Company M.T., Royal Army Service Corps, B.E.F.

Bashall, Corpl. J. T. ... ... 1904-6 *a*

83rd Company M.T., Royal Army Service Corps, B.E.F.

*Bass-Thomson, Lieut. L. D. ... 1897-1901 *b*

R.N.V.R., Motor Boat Reserve; Légion d'Honneur; Order of the White Eagle (Serbian); Order of the Crown of Italy; and the Croix de Guerre.

Bathurst, Major A. H. (Retired) 1886-90 *a*

Dep. Asst. Adjt. Gen., Eastern Command.

BATHURST, Capt. C., M.P. ... 1883-6 *a*

Royal Engineers (Special Reserve), R. Monmouthshire; Asst. Military Secretary, S. Command.

†BATTERSBY, Capt. E. M. ... 1899-1901 *d*

The Queen's Own (Royal West Kent Regiment), 3rd Bn.; killed at Neuve Chapelle, October 27th, 1914.

*BATTISHILL, Lieut. P. H. ... 1903-7 *d*

The Prince of Wales's Own (West Yorkshire Regiment), 4th Bn.; wounded, July 28th, 1918; M.C. and Bar.

†BAWDON, 2nd Lieut. R. H. ... 1909-13 *f*

The South Wales Borderers, 7th (S.) Bn.; died on Active Service, July 10th, 1915.

BAX, Cadet S. N. ... ... 1913-18 *c*

Officers Cadet Bn., Household Brigade.

*BAXTER, Capt. (a./Major) D. ... 1906-10 *b*

The Gloucester Regt, 1st Bn.; seriously wounded 1st battle of Ypres, October, 1914; attached Machine Gun Corps (1918), 14th Bn.; M.C.; mentioned in despatches (twice).

BAYLISS, Lieut. A. W. E. ... 1907-9 *a*

Royal Engineers (Territorial Force); 69th Div. Sig. Co., E. Anglian.

†BAYLY, 2nd Lieut. V. T. ... 1910-12 *d*

The Dorsetshire Regiment, 7th (S.) Bn.; killed, near Albert, May 7th, 1916.

BEADON, Naval Cadet R. ... 1913-16 *Prep.*

Osborne, 1916; Dartmouth, 1917, to Armistice.

Beale, Sergt. C. W. ... ... 1901-2 *b*
Royal Air Force.

†Bean, Lieut. C. R. C. ... ... 1905-8 *b*
The South Staffordshire Regt.; killed, near Ypres, October 26th, 1914.

*Beckett, Capt. W. E.... ... 1910-14 *c*
The Cheshire Regiment, 3rd Bn.; mentioned in despatches; G.S.O. 3rd Grade, 27th Division.

†*Beckton, Lieut. H. ... ... 1907-11 *d*
Royal Field Artillery; died 23rd September, 1919, of illness as a result of wounds; Croix de Guerre.

Beckton, S./Sergt. H. S. ... 1906-10 *b*
16th Canadian Infantry Bn. (Canadian Scottish); wounded April, 1915; transferred to Canadian Pay and Record Office.

Bell, 2nd Lieut. C. D.... ... 1905-7 *f*
The Northumberland Fusiliers.

Bellairs, Lieut. I. M. ... 1897-1900 *f*
R.N.A.S., 10th August, 1914; served in France and Belgium; Secret Service in Holland and Germany; 1916 and 1917, East Africa.

†Benbow, Pte. J. L. ... ... 1902-5 *b*
The Royal Fusiliers (City of London Regiment); killed in action, at the attack on Combles, September 15th, 1916.

†Benison, 2nd Lieut. E. W. ... 1903-8 *a*
Royal Garrison Artillery (T.), No. 3 Company, Dorsetshire; died of peritonitis at Weymouth, August 13th, 1915.

*Benet, Lieut.-Col. H. V. F. ... 1876-9 *b*

Lancashire Fusiliers (Reserve of Officers); G.S.O., 2nd Grade, War Office; C.B.E; Légion d'Honneur, Croix d'Officier; Order of St. Valdimir, 4th Class with swords and bow; of St. Stanislaus, 2nd Class with swords; of St. Anne, 2nd Class with swords.

Bennet, Col. F. W. ... ... 1862-7 *a*

Royal Engineers.

Bennett, Pte. D. ... ... 1900-5 *a*

Honourable Artillery Company, 1st Bn.

†Bennett, Sergt. B. C. ... ... 1905-7 *d*

Dorset Yeomanry (Queen's Own), 1st Bn.; killed in Palestine, May 4th, 1917.

*Bennett, Capt. G. ... ... 1906-11 *a*

Intelligence Corps (G.H.Q. Staff, France); formerly in Royal Army Service Corps; mentioned in despatches.

Bennett, Capt. and Hon. Major L. W. ... ... ... 1880-3 *b*

The Queen's (Royal West Surrey) Regiment, 9th (2nd Reserve) Bn.; employed at Depôt, Suffolk Regiment.

*Bennett, Lieut. M. C. ... 1903-6 *f*

The Herefordshire Regiment, 1st Bn.; 5th Company, Imp. Camel Corps, E.E.F.; mentioned in despatches.

†Bennett, Lieut. M. P. ... 1911-15 *g*

The Queen's (Royal West Surrey) Regiment, 2nd Bn.; died of wounds received near the Menin Road, October 8th, 1917.

*BENNETT, Capt. W. ... ... 1905-8 *a*
Royal Engineers; Signals, 9th Corps, Heavy Artillery; M.C.

†BENNETTS, Flight Sub-Lieut. E. A. 1909-13 *c*
R.N.A.S.; Formerly Lance-Corpl. in Cape Town Highlanders, South African Defence Force (Signalling Instructor); killed in an air battle, N.E. of Lens, August 17th, 1917.

*BENSLY, Capt. (temp. Major) The Rev. W. J. ... ... 1888-93 *a*, 1905-*Master*
1st United Provinces Horse, India, 1914-15; 7th Bn., Dorsetshire Regiment, 1915-16; 1st Bn., West Indian Regiment, 1916-19; served in India, Egypt, Sinai and Palestine; D.S.O.; mentioned in despatches.

BENSON, 2nd Lieut. T. G. ... 1912-18 *f*
Kings Own Yorkshire Light Infantry.

BENSTED, Corpl. F. H. ... ... 1909-12 *c*
Royal Engineers; Motor Cycle Despatch Rider, 28th Division, Signal Company; invalided out.

BENSTED, Driver J. A. ... ... 1912-13 *c*
Honourable Artillery Company; (965) 2/1st 'B' Battery, 126th Brigade, R.F.A., B.E.F.

*BENT, Lieut. H. K. R. ... ... 1911-13 *g*
Inns of Court O.T.C. and Royal Field Artillery; served in France, gassed and wounded; discharged permanently unfit, March, 1918; M.C.

BERKELEY, Lieut. M. H. ... 1913-17 *c*
Indian Army; Ghurkha Rifles, 1/7th Bn.; served in Persia.

BERRYMAN, Capt. F. H. ... 1883-6 *a*

Royal Garrison Artillery (late Cardigan R. F. Reserve, A.).

*BEST, Comdr. The Hon. M. R. ... 1887-90 *Prep.*

R.N.; D.S.O., M.V.O.

BERTRAM, Capt. J. N. ... ... 1902-5 *f*

The Royal Scots (Lothian Regiment), 7th Bn.

*BESANT, Major R. E. ... ... 1896-8 *c*

Commandant, R. A. Reinforcement Camp, Fifth Army, France; previously served as private in Universities and Public Schools Bns., Royal Fusiliers; Commission in 10th (S.) Bn., Loyal North Lancashire Regiment, October, 1914, to April, 1916; D.T.M.O. attached to 37th Divisional Artillery Staff to December, 1916; Chief Instructor, Trench Mortar School, Fifth Army, to June, 1918; mentioned in despatches (thrice).

†BETTS, 2nd Lieut. C. C. ... 1913-17 *c*

Royal Air Force; killed, April 17th, 1918, (in the Aegean Sea owing to engine trouble) while on his way to bomb the Goeben.

*BETTS, Capt. E. B. C. ... 1911-14 *c*

Royal Air Force; D.S.C., D.F.C.; Croix de Guerre with palms (French).

BEWES, 2nd Lieut. H. T. ... 1901-6 *a*

The Dorsetshire Regiment, 3rd Bn. (Reserve).

BIENEMAN, Rev. G. A. ... 1888-92 *Master*

Chaplain to 30th Casualty Clearing Station.

BIRCH, Major D. P. L. ... ... 1877-9 *a*
Royal Garrison Artillery (Reserve of Officers).

*BIRD, Major A. ... ... 1869-72 *d*
R.A.M.C. (T.F.); O. i/c Troops, Ambulance Transport, St. Denis; mentioned for War Services.

BIRD, Capt. C. E. H. ... ... 1904-5 *a*
Royal Army Service Corps; O.C., R.A.S.S., 68th Brigade, Royal Garrison Artillery.

*BIRKS, a./Capt. (temp. Major) E. R. 1893-7 *a*
West Riding Brigade, R.F.A. (T.); O.C. 3/3rd Brigade, June 1st, 1915, to February 28th, 1916; C.R.O. 33rd Regimental District, June 1st, 1916, to March 25th, 1918; Overseas, May, 1918; commanding a P.O.W. Company in France since October, 1918; mentioned in despatches.

BITTLESTON, Lieut. D. H. ... 1908-11 *c&T.*
R.F.A., 'A' Battery, 88th Brigade; served in France, September to November, 1915; with Salonika Force, November, 1915, to January, 1919.

BLACKMORE, Bombadier H. C. ... 1884-90 *Price*
Royal Garrison Artillery.

†BLAIR, 2nd Lieut. G. Y. ... 1908-13 *b*
R.F.A., 10th Division; killed in France, July 24th, 1915.

BLAKELEY, Lieut. H. P. ... 1914-16 *g*
Royal Air Force; Cadet, April, 1917; 2nd Lieut., July, 1917; Lieutenant, March, 1918; France, 46th Squadron, October, 1917; Rochford (Essex), 61st Squadron, Home Defence, August, 1918; Demobilised, March, 1919.

†BLANDFORD, Pte. C. E. ... 1910-13 *a*

The King's Royal Rifle Corps, 22nd Bn.; attached 5th Field Survey Bn., Royal Engineers; killed in France, July 20th, 1918.

BLANDFORD, 2nd Lieut. J. V. ... 1913-15 *a*

Royal Air Force; on Active Service with H.M.S. 'Royal Sovereign' in the North Sea.

†BLENCOWE, Capt. E. C. B. ... 1896-9 *c*

The Dorsetshire Regiment, 6th (S.) Bn.; killed on the Bluff, near Hill 60, Ypres Salient, February 16th, 1916.

†BLIGH, 2nd Lieut. E. ... ... 1908-13 *f*

The East Lancashire Regiment, 3rd Bn. (Reserve); attached 2nd Bn.; killed at Fromelles, May 9th, 1915.

BLIGH, Capt. W., M.D., B.Sc. (Lond.), M.R.C.S., L.R.C.P. ... 1880-4 *d*

R.A.M.C.; No. 9, Rouen, December, 1916 to September, 1917; No. 38, Stationary, Genoa, August, 1918; then to Caesar's Camp and No. 11, General, Genoa.

*BOLTON, Lieut. E. J. ... ... 1910-15 *b*

The Dorsetshire Regiment, 3rd Bn. (Reserve); attached 5th Bn.; M.C.

†BOND, Capt. C. G. ... 1892-1900 *a*

The Duke of Edinburgh's (Wiltshire Regiment); Adjt. 1/4th Bn. (T.); killed at Givenchy, November 25th, 1915.

*BOND, Lieut. E. F. ... ... 1900-5 *a*

111th Siege Battery, Royal Garrison Artillery; M.C.

*BOND, Lieut.-Col. J. H. R. ... 1884-7 *c*
R.A.M.C.; mentioned in despatches (thrice); C.B.E., D.S.O.

BOURKE, Lieut.-Col. H. B., D.S.O. 1871-2 *b*
West India Regiment; retired; (late 1st); served as Draft Conducting Officer.

*BOUSFIELD, Lieut.-Col. H. R. ... 1877-8 *a*
Retired, 1913; Chairman Durban Recruiting Committee, 1914-18; Chairman Re-employment Soldier's Committee, 1917; Member Central Advisory Board, (S.A.) Records and Re-employment, 1918; C.M.G.

BOWEN, Major A. G. W. ... 1876-80 *d*
Royal Army Medical Corps; Military Convalescent Hospital, Crownhill Hutments, near Plymouth.

†BOWEN, Lieut. E. G. A. ... 1907-11 *f*
On coast defence at outbreak of war; went to Flanders with 71st Heavy Battery, June, 1915; became Observer, in No. 6 Squadron, R.F.C., in August, 1915; passed as Pilot, May, 1916, and joined 22nd Squadron on Somme front; killed, fighting in the air, between Thilloy and Le Barque, September 8th, 1916.

*BOWKER, Major W. J., D.S.O. ... 1880-5 *d*
Prince Albert's (Somerset Light Infantry), 2nd Bn.; C.M.G.

BOWMAN, Capt. J. H. ... 1897-1900 *b*
The Durham Light Infantry, 2/7th Bn. (T.); also served with North Russian Expeditionary Force, 1918-19.

*BOYD, Capt. J. E. M. ... ... 1889-91 *f*
Royal Army Medical Corps; M.C.

BOYNE, Capt. L. L. ... ... 1903-5 *c*

The Royal Sussex Regiment, 3rd Bn. (Reserve).

*BRADFORD, Capt. and Adjt. J. P. ... 1900-2 *c*

Royal Army Service Corps, Base Mechanical Transport Depôt (Northern), France; mentioned in despatches.

BRADFORD, Major L. B. ... 1902-4 *c*

R.F.A.; Dorsetshire Battery, 3rd Wessex Brigade(T.); commanding 1103rd Battery, 227th Brigade, R.F.A., stationed at Secunderabad, August, 1917; commanding 'A' Battery, 312th Brigade, R.F.A., 62nd Division, B.E.F., France; gassed, September 17th, 1918.

BRAKSPEAR, Capt. A. R. ... 1885-8 *a*

Oxford and Bucks Light Infantry, 4th Bn.; invalided out, July, 1916.

BRAMALL, Capt. E. G. ... ... 1908-12 *f*

The Royal Sussex Regiment, 5th (Cinque Ports) Bn. (T.).

BRAMALL, Major E. H. ... ... 1903-8 *f*

R.F.A.; served in Egypt; Staff Capt., 19th Div. Artillery, April to July, 1916; commanding D/86 Brigade, July to September, 1916; invalided home, September, 1916, to November, 1917; commanding C/86 Brigade, November to February, 1918; invalided home, February, 1918; attached Officer, A.G. 2 (O), War Office.

*BRASSEY, Capt. H. R. ... ... 1906-9 *c*

Royal Field Artillery, B/70th Brigade; M.C.

BRATBY, Lance-Corpl. G. S. ... 1892-4 *d*

The Gloucestershire Regiment, 3rd (S.) Bn. ; gassed and shellshocked, July, 1916 ; discharged, February, 1918.

*BRATBY, a./Capt. S. H. ... ... 1892-5 *d*

Royal Army Service Corps, 3/1st East Lancashire Division ; served in Mesopotamia, October, 1916, to August, 1918 ; mentioned in despatches (twice) ; M.B.E.

BREWIS, 2nd Lieut. E. ... ... 1913-16 *a*

Royal Army Service Corps.

BRIDGE, 2nd Lieut. D. E. ... 1902-3 *a*

H.Q., 402nd M.T. Company, Royal Army Service Corps. Canadian Corps, Seige Park, B.E.F.

BRIDGES, Major T. McG. ... 1886-90 *a*

The Loyal North Lancashire Regiment, 2nd Bn.

†BRINE, Lieut. E. L. ... ... 1905-9 *a*

The Hampshire Regiment, 3/4th Bn. ; attached 1/4th Bn., Indian Expeditionary Force ; served in Mesopotamia ; died of enteric at Hamadam, Persia, September 24th, 1918.

BROADMEAD, Bt. Col. H. ... 1872-9 *a*

Essex Regiment.

†BROADRICK, Major F. B. D. ... 1881-4 *f*

R.F.A. ; died in hospital at Harve, April 19th, 1918.

†BROOKE, Capt. G. D. ... ... 1905-8 *c*

The Suffolk Regiment, 7th (S.) Bn. ; killed, July 3rd, 1916, at Ovillers-la-Boiselle.

BROOKMAN, Capt. O. J. R. ... 1897-1900 *c*
Royal Army Service Corps; Mechanical Transport.

BROOKS-KING, Lieut. M. ... 1908-13 *c*
Prince Albert's (Somerset Light Infantry), 2/5th Bn. (T.); served in India from December, 1914; Signalling Officer to the Brigade.

BROWN, Capt. B. W., M.B. ... 1899-1904 *T.*
R.A.M.C.

BROWN, Lieut. C. A. ... ... 1900-6 *T.*
R.F.A.

BROWN, Lieut. C. B. ... ... 1898-1904 *b*
Unattached List (T.F.); Christ's Hospital O.T.C.

BROWN, 2nd Lieut. E. F. ... 1905-9 *d*
Royal Engineers; Railway Operative Department; served in Salonika.

BROWN, Capt. I. A. ... ... 1905-9 *T.*
The Royal Warwickshire Regiment, 2nd Bn.

†BROWN, Lieut. O. ... ... 1902-6 *T.*
4th (Royal Irish) Dragoon Guards; attached from 7th Hariana Lancers; killed in France. April 24th, 1915.

BROWN, 2nd Lieut. M. E. ... 1914-17 *g*
Royal Air Force; Cadet, October 3rd, 1917 (Wendover, St. Leonard's and Hastings); 2nd Lieut., June, 1918; France, 102 Squadron; Hospital, October, 1919; Demobilised, November, 1919.

BROWN, Lieut. W. F. ... ... 1914-16 *c*
Royal Military College, Sandhurst, and 18th (Q.M.O.) Hussars; Secunderabad, India.

*BROWNE-MASON, Lieut.-Col. H.O.B. 1885-9 *a*
R.A.M.C.; taken prisoner at fall of Kut; repatriated to India, September, 1916; mentioned in despatches (twice); D.S.O.

BRUTTON, Major G. K. H. ... 1882-5 *b*
Headquarters Chinese Labour Corps.

BUCHANAN, Lieut.-Col. J. B.W., M.B. 1877-8 *b*
R.A.M.C.

BUCHANAN-WOLLASTON, 2nd Lieut. H. J. ... ... 1896-9 *a*
DorsetYeomanry (Queen's Own), 2nd Bn.

*BUCKLE, Major-Gen. C. R. ... 1875-80 *c*
Royal Artillery; C.B., C.M.G., D.S.O.; Légion d'Honneur, Order of Crown of Italy, Order of Military Savoy, Order of Leopold 1st, Order of Leopold 2nd, Croix de Guerre; mentioned in despatches ten times.

BUCK, Capt. F. C. W. ... ... 1906-7 *d*
Royal Army Service Corps; attached 93rd Brigade, R.G.A.; served in France from December 28th, 1914.

BULL, Capt. W. R. ... ... 1902-7 *f*
Royal Army Service Corps.

*BULLEN, Lieut. D. B. F. ... 1900-4 *c*
Canadian Infantry, 8th Bn. (90th Winnipeg Rifles); mentioned in despatches.

Bullock, Lieut. J. C. C. ... 1913-16 *g*

18th King George's Own Lancers, Indian Army, B.E.F., France.

Bullock, Lieut. P. C. ... ... 1914-17 *g*

Indian Army; Cadet College, Quetta; 14th Jat Lancers; O.C. Veterinary Hospital, Bareilly.

Bunbury, Major W. C. H. ... 1882-5 *a*

The Gordon Highlanders, 9th Bn.; served at Depôt, Royal Scots (Lothian Regiment), August 4th, 1914, to January 10th, 1915; Command Signalling Officer, Scotland, till November 1st, 1916; in India, January, 1917, to December, 1918; appointed Cantonment Magistrate, Murree, April 4th, 1917.

Bunting, Sapper G. F. C. ... 1903-8 *f*

Hants (Fortress) Royal Engineers (T.).

Bundock, Capt. C. S. ... ... 1882-5 *a*

Australian Remounts, in Egypt, 1915-16 (Disbanded); Australian Munition Workers' Department, London, 1917 and 1918.

Burgess, Pte. E. H. ... ... 1903-7 *a*

7th and 11th Bns., The Royal Fusiliers (City of London Regiment); badly wounded at Cambrai, October, 1918, B.E.F.

†Burgess, 2nd Lieut. P. G. ... 1903-8 *a*

The Queen's (Royal West Surrey) Regiment, 8th (S.) Bn.; died, October 13th, 1915, a prisoner at Douai, of wounds received at Loos, September 25th.

*BURT, Major A. E. ... ... 1906-11 *c*
The Oxfordshire and Buckinghamshire Light Infantry, 8th (S.) Bn., Pioneers; mentioned in despatches (twice); D.S.O.

*BURT-SMITH, Capt. B. ... ... 1910-12 *a*
The London Regiment, 1/6th (City of London) Bn. (Rifles); M.C. and Bar.

BUTLER, 2nd Lieut. A. H. ... 1908-11 *a*
The Queen's Own (Royal West Kent Regiment), 3/4th Bn. (T.).

†CAMPBELL, 2nd Lieut. D. G. ... 1901-4 *b*
A. Imp. F.; 1st Australian Division, 3rd Infantry Brigade, 11th Bn.; served in Gallipoli; killed at Mouquet Farm, September 3rd, 1916.

†CAPEL-CURE, Capt. B. A. ... 1907-10 *a*
The Gloucestershire Regiment, 2nd Bn.; died of wounds, Bala-zir, Salonika, October, 1916.

CAPEL-CURE, 2nd Lieut. L. H. ... 1903-8 *a*
The Prince of Wales's (North Staffordshire Regiment), 3rd Bn. (Reserve).

CARDEW, 2nd Lieut. W. G. ... 1898-1903 *a*
The Hampshire Regiment, 15th Bn., B.E.F., France.

†CARD, 2nd Lieut. S. H. ... 1899-1903
Prince Albert's (Somerset Light Infantry), 1st Bn.; slightly wounded, April 9th, 1917, and killed next day, near Fampoux, in first battle of Arras.

*CAREY, Bt. Lieut.-Col. A. B. ... 1887-9 *d*
Royal Engineers; R.M. Engineer Unit, R.N. Division; C.M.G.; mentioned in despatches (4 times); D.S.O.

CAREY, Capt. R. B. ... ... 1913-16 *d*
Royal Air Force.

CAREY, 2nd Lieut. C. O'D. ... 1901-8 *f*
Indian Army Reserve of Officers; 3/2nd (Queen Victoria's Own) Rajput Light Infantry (Allahabad); served with 2/10th Jats till August 16th, 1918, (Jhausi).

CAREY, Major F. C. S. ... 1897-1901 *a*
Royal Army Ordnance Department.

CAREY, Lieut. G. M. ... ... { 1886-91 *f* / 1897-*Master* }
Unattached List (T.F.), Sherborne O.T.C. (Physical Training).

CAREY, Major P. G. ... ... 1896-9 *f*
31st Punjabis; served in Mesopotamia.

*CAREY, Capt. R. O'D. ... ... 1905-10 *f*
The Duke of Wellington's (West Riding Regiment), 2nd Bn.; taken prisoner; returned, January, 1919; mentioned in despatches (twice).

*CARR, Lieut. A. W. ... ... 1907-11 *a*
5th (Royal Irish) Lancers; mentioned in despatches.

CARR, Lieut. P. G. ... ... 1911-14 *a*
7th (Princess Royal's) Dragoon Guards, (serving with 4th Reserve Regiment of Cavalry); invalided out, December, 1918.

†*CARR-ELLISON, a./Capt. O. F. C. 1909-14 *b*
The Northumberland Fusiliers, Special Reserve Bn., from October, 1914, and, later, 2nd Bn.; served in France, from June, 1915; then with the Salonika Force until July, 1918; returned to France and was killed there, October 4th, 1918; Order of the White Eagle (5th Class); mentioned in despatches.

Carr-Ellison, C. F. C. ... ... 1915-18 *b*
Gentleman Cadet, Royal Military Academy, Woolwich.

Carrington, 2nd Lieut. H. B. ... 1901-6 *f*
Royal Army Service Corps (M.T.); served in France.

†Carrington, Capt. H. E. ... 1899-1905 *f*
The Hampshire Regiment, 15th (S.) Bn.; killed in France, at capture of Flers (Somme), September 15th, 1916.

Carus-Wilson, Capt. M. M. ... 1908-13 *a*
The Dorsetshire Regiment, 1/4th Bn.(T.); served in India and Mesopotamia from December, 1914; on Staff as Record Officer, at Basra.

†Caruthers-Little, Capt. A. W. P. ... ... 1899-1903 *b*
The Dorsetshire Regiment, 2nd Bn.; Adjt. 5th (S.) Bn.; killed at the Dardanelles, August 7th or 8th, 1915.

*Caruthers-Little, Major R. J. ... 1901-4 *b*
The Gloucestershire Regiment, 1/5th Bn. (T.); served in France, Egypt and Palestine; attached 1st Garrison Bn. Northants Regiment; wounded; mentioned in despatches.

Catt, Lieut. N. ... ... 1908-12 *a*
R.F.A., 417th Battery; served with 42nd Battery, in France.

Caudwell, 2nd Lieut. F. W. H. 1912-16 *f*
The Oxfordshire and Buckinghamshire Light Infantry.

Chaffey, Capt. R. S. C. ... 1885-9 *Price*
Territorial Force Reserve; Infantry.

*CHAFFEY, Col. R. A., V.D. ... 1868-73 *b*
Commanding Canterbury Military District (No. 2); A.D.C. to Governor General, 1916; C.B.E.

*CHALKLEY, Capt. R. ... ... 1911-14 *d*
R.F.A., D/159th Brigade, 35th Division; served in Gallipoli and France; mentioned in despatches (twice); D.C.M.

CHANDLER, Capt. G. P. W. ... 1913-17 *f*
Royal Air Force.

*CHAPMAN, Capt. H. R. ... 1895-1900 *f*
Alexandra Princess of Wales's Own Yorkshire Regiment, 5th Bn. (T.); mentioned in despatches.

†CHATTERIS, Capt. T. B. ... 1899-1900 *c*
The Sherwood Foresters (Nottingham and Derbyshire Regiment), Special Reserve; killed at Hooge, August 9th, 1915.

CHEATLE, Capt. C. T. ... ... 1894-8 *c*
R.A.M.C.; served in Egypt.

*CHESTER-MASTER, 2nd Lieut. A. G. 1903-9 *T.*
Armoured Car Division, (East Africa); M.B.E.; mentioned in despatches.

*CHETHAM-STRODE, Capt. R. W. ... 1910-13 *b*
The Border Regiment, 3rd Bn. (Reserve), attached 2nd Bn.; since April, 1918, attached 18th Bn., Tank Corps; M.C.

*CHEVALLIER, Lieut. C. ... ... 1912-15 *f*
The Hampshire Regiment, 14th (S.) Bn.; mentioned in despatches.

CHICHESTER, Lieut. O. ... ... 1888-92 *d*
The Devonshire Regiment, 6th Bn. (T.).

CHICHESTER, Pte. A. R. ... 1893-6 *d*
The Royal Fusiliers (City of London Regiment), 9th Bn.; wounded at Ypres, July 31st, 1917.

†CHICHESTER, Capt. R. G. I. ... 1887-91 *f*
The Highland Light Infantry, 2nd Bn.; killed near Zonnebecke, Belgium, November 13th, 1914.

*CHURCH, Lieut.-Col. A. J. B. ... 1880-6 *b*
Staff Paymaster, Army Pay Department; C.M.G.; mentioned in despatches.

CHURCHILL, Lieut. W. F. ... 1894-5 *c*
The London Regiment, 3/7th (City of London) Bn.

CLAPIN, temp. Capt. A. C. ... 1880-8 *T.*
Attached Special Service with the 'Service Sanitaire Militaire', Armée des Vosges, November, 1914, till May, 1915; Capt., O.C. No. 6 Company, Kent A.S.C., M.T. (T.).

†CLAPTON, 2nd Lieut. A. ... ... 1907-12 *f*
The Royal Fusiliers (City of London Regiment), 32nd Bn.; wounded and missing in France, September 5th, 1916; presumed killed.

†*CLARK, Capt. H. C. ... ... 1896-8 *a*
Royal Wiltshire (Prince of Wales's Own Royal Regiment), B. Squadron; died of wounds received in action in France, February 7th, 1918; M.C.

CLARK, Col. P. T. ... ... 1868-73 *c*
Late C.O. 1st Bn. Oxford Light Infantry, (retired); Staff Captain for instructional duties.

CLARKE, Lieut. A. B. ... .. 1908-10 *Prep.*

1914, H.M.S. Irresistible, which ship was mined in Dardanelles; served on H.M.S. Inflexible, present at Battle of Jutland; finally, H.M. Destroyer, Lucifer.

CLARKE, Lieut. H. P. ... ... 1910-15 *b*

R.F.A.; attached 2/24th T.M.B., B.E.F.

CLARKE, Pte. M. N. ... ... 1912-13 *T.*

Inns of Court, O.T.C.

†CLARKE, Pte. W. W. E. M. ... 1911-13 *g*

The London Regiment, 1/4th (County of London) Bn. (London Scottish); Despatch Carrier; killed, July 1st, 1916.

†CLATWORTHY, 2nd Lieut. T. E. 1899-1901 *b*

Indian Army; 37th Dogras; killed in Mesopotamia, January 6th, 1916.

COATH, Lieut. R. D. ... ... 1907-10 *a*

Scottish Horse, 2/2nd Bn.; attached Royal Air Force.

COCHRANE, Lieut.-Col. G. L. ... 1887-91 *f*

The Durham Light Infantry, 3rd Bn.

COCHRANE, Lieut.-Col. J. E. C. J., D.S.O. ... ... 1884-6 *b*

R.F.A. (Reserve of Officers) Commanding Ammunition Column, New Zealand Artillery.

CODRINGTON, 2nd Lieut. K. de B. 1913-17 *c*

Indian Army; 33rd Queen Victoria's Own Light Cavalry.

COFFIN, Capt. A. S. ... ... 1900-4 *c*

Indian Army; 28th Punjabis.

Cole, Pte. C. H. ... ... 1901-6 *a*
London Regiment; 2/28th Bn.

Cole, Rev. G. L. ... ... 1900-6 *a*
Army Chaplains' Department.

Colebrook, Capt. L. F. ... 1909-12 *a*
The King's Own (Royal Lancashire Regiment), 8th (S.) Bn.; transferred Administrative Captain, Royal Air Force, April 18th, 1918.

*Coleman, Capt. G. D. ... ... 1907-11 *a*
The Norfolk Regiment, 3rd Bn.; mentioned War Services.

Coleridge, D. W. R. ... ... 1909 *b*
Public Schools' Bn. Royal Fusiliers and Intelligence Staff; served in France.

Colley, 2nd Lieut. A. S. ... 1913-18 *g*
R.M.A.Woolwich and 72nd Battery, 38th Brigade, Royal Field Artillery.

*Collier, 2nd Lieut. A. C. ... 1909-14 *b*
Royal Flying Corps, 3rd Squadron; prisoner; mentioned for gallantry whilst prisoner of war.

Collier, Lieut.-Col. W., M.D. ... 1871-4 *b*
Royal Army Medical Corps.

*Collins, 2nd Lieut. G. R. G. ... 1910-13 *a*
R.F.A., 33rd Divl. Artillery, 'A' Battery, 166th Brigade; mentioned in despatches.

Collot, Lieut. H. G. ... ... 1910-12 *a*
The Welsh Regiment, 3rd Bn.

†Collot, 2nd Lieut. T. A. ... 1908-12 *a*
Princess Charlotte of Wales's (Royal Berkshire Regiment), 6th (S.) Bn.; killed at the Battle of the Somme, July 1st, 1916.

Colmore, Major H. ... ... 1896-1900 *f*

7th (Queen's Own) Hussars; A.D.C., Personal Staff of Commander-in-Chief; attached 12th Lancers.

Comerford, Major R. H. J. ... 1876-9 *a*

(retired) 16th (County of London) Bn. The London Regiment, Queen's (Westminster) Rifles, T.F.

Cooke, 2nd Lieut. F. H. ... 1902-5 *c*

R.N. Division.

Cooper, Pte. A. ... ... 1896-1900 *a*

The London Regiment, 1st Bn. London Rifle Brigade; resigned in October, 1914, to take up duties in India.

Cooper, Lieut. A. H. ... ... 1903-7 *b*

Railway Transport Officer; severely wounded in France, November, 1915.

Cooper, Lieut. H. F. L. ... 1909-10 *d*

The Hampshire Regiment, 4th Bn. (T.).

Coote, Capt. M. C. ... ... 1900-2 *c*

Indian Army; 107th Pioneers.

Corfe, a./Sergt.-Major C. ... 1906-11 *a*

Canadian Engineers.

*Cornish, Lieut. G. M. ... ... 1907-13 *a*

Grenadier Guards, 3rd Bn.; M.C.

Costley-White, Capt. The Rev. H. 1901-3 *Master*

Liverpool College O.T.C.

Cottam, Lieut. A. C. S. ... 1904-7 *a*

Royal Air Force; Dental Officer; No. 1 School Aerial Gunnery, Hythe and No. 8 Aircraft Acceptance Park, Lympne.

COTTER, Cadet H. ... ... 1914-18 *Prep.*
R.N.; Naval Cadet at Osborne.

COURTAULD, Capt. J. R. ... 1888-9 *d*
The Essex Regiment, 2/5th Bn. (T.).

COUSINS, Lieut. W. D. P. ... 1909-11 *a*
The Dorsetshire Regiment; enlisted in Public Schools and University Corps, 1914; 2nd Lieut., 3rd Dorsets, May 20th, 1915; Lieut., July 1st, 1917; served with 1st Dorsets and 6th Dorsets in France, with 2/4th Dorsets and I.A. in Egypt and Palestine.

COWELL, 2nd Lieut. R. G. ... 1913-16 *g*
The Bedfordshire Regiment, 8th Bn.

COX, 2nd Lieut. A. B. ... ... 1907-11 *c*
The Northamptonshire Regiment, 7th (S.) Bn.

CRAVEN, Lieut. J. L. A. ... 1910-14 *c*
The Duke of Cornwall's Light Infantry, 3rd Bn. (Reserve).

CRAVEN, Lieut. N. F. de la B. 1898-1900 *b*
Royal Army Ordnance Department.

†CRAWHALL, Lieut. N. G. ... 1907-12 *a*
The Manchester Regiment, 1st Bn.; killed July 7th, 1916, in Mametz Wood, France.

CRAWHALL-WILSON, 2nd Lieut. C.L. 1911-15 *c*
The Bedfordshire Regiment, 5th & 11th Bns. (T.).

CRICHTON, Capt. E. C. ... ... 1903-7 *a*
Royal Army Medical Corps; attached 1/5th Bn. Suffolks, E.E.F.

†CRICHTON, 2nd Lieut. A. G. ... 1900-4 *a*

Enlisted in Seaforth Highlanders at Vancouver at outbreak of war; permitted to go to Dublin and enlist in 'D' Co., 7th (S.) Bn. Royal Dublin Fusiliers; made Lance-corpl., December, 1914, Corpl., January, 1915, gazetted 2nd Lieut., R.D.F., April, 1915; missing, believed killed, 16th August, 1915, Suvla Bay.

†CROFT-SMITH, Lieut. E. S. ... 1906-9 *a*

The King's Royal Rifle Corps, 4th Bn.; missing, May 10th, 1915; assumed killed.

CRONSHAW, Lieut. T. J. ... ... 1904-9 *a*

Nigerian Field Force, B/3 Company.

†CROSBY, 2nd Lieut. A. B. L. ... 1910-13 *d*

The Durham Light Infantry, 5th Bn.; died of wounds in Arras, France, April 28th, 1917.

CROUCHER, Pte. A. A. ... ... 1914-16 *d*

Somerset Light Infantry, 3rd Bn.; and Hampshire Regiment, 2nd Bn.; served in France.

*CROWDY, Sergt. A. A. G. ... 1902-7 *a*

The Rifle Brigade (The Prince Consort's Own), 12th Bn.; formerly Lieutenant in Royal Army Service Corps, but invalided out, through ill-health, November 16th, 1917; D.C.M.

CROWTHER, Lieut. A. D. ... 1909-12 *b*

Royal Army Service Corps; served with Egyption Expeditionary Force; G.H.Q., May to June, 1916; Camel Corps, July, 1916, to August, 1917; R.A.S.C. (H.T.), August, 1917, to April, 1918; R.A.F., (scout pilot), April, 1918, to April, 1919.

CRUMP, Capt. G. H. ... ... 1912-13 *Master*
The Essex Regiment, 4th Bn. (T.).

*CUNNINGHAM, Bt. Major (a./Lieut.-Col.) C.C. ... ... 1894-9 *f*
In Command, 2nd/107th Pioneers, Indian Army; in 1914, Brigade-Major 1st Naval Brigade; 1915, 12th Pioneers (The Khelat-i-Ghilzie Regiment); G.S.O., 3rd Grade, 24th Division; 1917, in Command, The Duke of Cambridge's Own (Middlesex Regiment); wounded; mentioned in despatches; D.S.O.

*CUNNINGHAM, Major J. F., F.R.C.S. 1889-94 *f*
R.A.M.C.; Ophthalmic Specialist, B.E.F.; O.B.E.

CURME, Lieut.-Col. D. E. ... 1887-9 *c*
R.A.M.C.

†CUSTANCE, Surgeon G. W. M. 1896-1901 *c*
H.M.S. Hawke; drowned on H.M.S. Hawke, October 14th, 1914.

*CUTHBERT, Capt. R. F. ... ... 1888-94 *a*
The Oxfordshire and Buckinghamshire Light Infantry; 4th Bn. (T.); wounded November 13th, 1917; M.C.

DALE, Lieut. C. B. M. ... ... 1908-12 *a*
The Northumberland Fusiliers, 2/4th Bn. (T.); Royal Air Force, served in Mesopotamia with 30th Squadron, afterwards in Egypt.

*DAMMERS, Comdr. C. M. ... 1886-89 *Prep.*
R.N.; 1914, H.M.S. Ganges; 1917, H.M.S. Europa, and H.M.S. Valkgrie, mine sweeping in Eastern Mediterranean; D.S.O., Chevalier of Légion of Honneur.

Dammers, Capt. E. H. F. ... 1905-9 *a*
The Dorsetshire Regiment, 2/4th Bn.(T.).

*Dammers, Capt. (temp. Major) G. M. 1892-7 *a*
Dorset Yeomanry (Queen's Own), 1st Bn. (T.F.); M.C., D.S.O.

Dandridge, Capt. A. H. ... 1902-4 *d*
Honourable Artillery Company, 'A' Battery; gassed at Doignies, France, March 21st, 1918.

†Dandridge, Lance-Corpl. A. P. 1902-1905 *d*
The King's Royal Rifle Corps, 20th Bn.; died of wounds in hospital at Abbeville on August 6th, 1916.

†Dandridge, Lieut. W. L. ... 1908-12 *d*
R.A.M.C.; died in hospital on October 5th, 1918, from wounds received in action on October 3rd, 1918; interred at Haringhe, Belgium.

Daniel, Lieut. A. H. ... ... 1902-6 *c*
Australian Imperial Expeditionary Force, 3rd Bn., 1st Infantry Brigade.

Davie, Cadet K. M. ... ... 1914-18 *b*
Household Brigade, Officer Cadet Bn.

*Davies, Lieut. E. H. ... ... 1906-7 *a*
1st Australian Contingent; 3rd Field Company, Divisional Engineers; transferred to 15th Field Company, 1916; served in Egypt, Gallipoli and France; M.C.

Davies, Capt. H. C. A. ... 1910-14 *a*
The South Wales Borderers, 6th (S.) Bn. (Pioneers).

*DAVIES, Major O. H. ... 1898-1902 *f*
Royal Garrison Artillery; 23rd Siege Battery, B.E.F.; M.C.

DAVIES, Lieut. W. W. N. ... 1913-15 *a*
13th Hussars; served in Mesopotamia.

DAVIS, Major E. ... ... 1903-*Master*
Unattached List (T.F.); Commanding Sherborne School O.T.C.

*DAVSON, Major H. J. H. ... 1895-8 *c*
Indian Army; 82nd Punjabis; served in France, Mesopotamia and Palestine; D.S.O.; mentioned in despatches, three times.

DAWSON, Capt. C. W. ... ... 1895-7 *c*
Royal Garrison Artillery.

DAY, Capt. A. B. H. ... ... 1908-10 *a*
Royal Field Artillery, 215th Brigade; formerly in 1/2nd Hampshire Battery, 1st Wessex Brigade, R.F.A. (T.); served in India and Mesopotamia.

DAY, Lieut. A. J. ... ... 1871-4 *a*
Late 2nd Lieut. Middlesex Yeomanry; assistant Recruiting Officer, 35th R.D. Recruiting Area, Chichester; Lieut., 434th Agricultural Labour Corps; Commandant, Bognor Division, National Reserve.

DAY, Lieut.-Col. C. R. L. ... 1885-90 *c*
Commanding 2/5th Bn. (T.), The Hampshire Regiment; served in India, December, 1914; on Staff, 9th Division, Ootacamund, April-July, 1916; Egypt, April, 1917; Palestine, till July, 1917; transferred, from illness, T.F. Reserve, November, 1917.

DAY, Lieut.-Col. D. A. L. ... 1887-92 *c*

The Royal Warwickshire Regiment, 1st Bn.; wounded at battle of Le Cateau; prisoner of war, in hospital at Cambria, and at Hanover Hospital; interned at Celle Schlosz, Halle, Augustabad and Heidelberg; transferred to Holland, January 22nd, 1917; repatriated, November 16th, 1918.

*DEACON, Bt. Lieut.-Col. H. R. G. 1886-9 *b*

The Connaught Rangers, 1st Bn.; attached Highland Light Infantry; D.S.O. and Bar, Légion d'Honneur, Chevalier; mentioned in despatches (three times); served in Mesopotamia.

DE BURGH, 2nd Lieut. U. ... 1913-18 *a*

Indian Army, Corps of Guides, 3rd Bn..

*DE COURCY-IRELAND, Capt. and Adjt. G. B. ... ... ... 1909-13 *a*

The King's Royal Rifle Corps, 16th Bn. (attached 5th Bn.); M.C., M.V.O., 1914-15 Mons Star.

DE COURCY-IRELAND, Lieut. L. K. 1911-14 *a*

The Devonshire Regiment, 11th (S.) Bn.; served in France with 1st Bn., May, 1916; wounded, July 24th, 1916, at Longueval (Somme); invalided out, Lieut. with Hon. rank, December 25th, 1917.

DENHAM, Lieut.-Col. L. S. ... 1889-92 *f*

The King's (Liverpool Regiment); Capt. Reserve of Officers Middlesex Regiment; commanding 19th (S.) Bn. (3rd City), The Duke of Cambridge's Own (Middlesex Regiment).

*DENIS DE VITRE, Lieut. E. C. ... 1911-15 *a*
Princess Charlotte of Wales's (Royal Berkshire Regiment), 1st Bn.; mentioned in despatches.

DE PASS, G. ... ... ... 1908-10 *f*
5th Highland Division Head Quarters, T.F.; Staff car driver.

DE PASS, Lieut. H. ... ... 1896-8 *c*
Royal Army Service Corps.

DERRICK, Capt. L. ... ... 1909-11 *d*
Prince Albert's (Somerset Light Infantry), 1/4th Bn. (T.).

DE SALIS, 2nd Lieut. R. A. ... 1912-15 *a*
Indian Army, 3rd Skinners Horse.

DE STEIGER, Gunner, F. ... 1905-8 *d*
Royal Garrison Artillery; served in France and Salonika with the 182nd S.A.S.A.C. (Pack Mule Ammunition Column), and in Palestine with the 379th Siege Battery.

DE WINTON, Major A. J. ... 1865-72 *a*
2nd Brecknockshire Bn. (T.), South Wales Borderers; O.C. 81st Labour Company, B.E.F.

DIXEY, Lieut. H. G. ... ... 1907-10 *f*
R.F.A.; N. Midland Brigade (T.).

DIXON, 2nd Lieut. M. D. ... 1913-18 *b*
Royal Engineers (Signal Depot).

*DIXON, Capt. W. A. ... ... 1905-7 *a*
The Duke of Edinburgh's (Wiltshire Regiment), 3rd (S.) Bn.; attached (1918) 51st Graduated Bn., The Queen's (Royal West Surrey) Regiment; wounded, Salonika, April 24th, 1917; M.C.

*DIXON, Capt. and Adjt. G. S. ... 1908-13 *b*

Private in The Buffs (East Kent Regiment), 4th Bn. (T.), August 20th, 1914, to October 29th, 1914; 2nd Lieut. 2/4th Buffs (T.), October 29th, 1914, to June 6th, 1915; Lieut. and Adjt., June 6th, 1915, to August 31st, 1915; Capt. and Adjt., September 1st, 1915, to September 25th, 1917; on demobilization of 2/4th Buffs in September, 1917, attached to 1st (S.) Bn. Royal Guernsey Light Infantry, in France, September 26th, 1917; Assistant Brigade Major on 86th Brigade Staff, 29th Division, November 3rd, 1917, to February 14th, 1918; wounded at Armentières, Battle of the Lys, April 4th, 1918; returned as Adjt. to 1st (S.) Bn. Royal Guernsey Light Infantry, July 30th, 1918; O.B.E.; mentioned in despatches.

*DONNE, Col. H. R. B., C.B. ... 1873-8 *f*

G.S.O. 2nd Grade, War Office; C.M.G.; mentioned in despatches.

DOUGLAS, Rev. E. C. ... 1899-1904 *T.*

Army Chaplains' Dept., attached 15th Bn. K.O.Y.L.I.; B.E.F.

DOUGLAS, Pte. K. J. ... ... 1894-9 *T.*

Nigerian Land Contingent.

DOUGLAS, Comdr. S. C. ... ... 1895-6 *Prep.*

1914-16, in command of Submarines, and subsequently in command H.M.S. Alecto, Submarines Depot Ship; 1916, in command H.M.S. Q iii; 1917, joined staff of Admiral Sir Lewis Bailey, K.C.B.

DOW, Sergt. W. I. ... ... 1902-7 *b*

Honourable Artillery Company.

Drake, 2nd Lieut. W. B. ... 1886-90 *b*
The Devonshire Regiment; Garrison Bn.

Drake-Cutcliffe, 2nd Lieut. B. H. H. ... ... ... 1913-15 *c*
The Devonshire Regiment; 1st Bn.

*Dreschfeld, Lieut. S. E. ... 1911-16 *d*
Royal Air Force; Air Force Cross.

*Drewe, Capt. A. S. ... ... 1906-7 *b*
The Leicestershire Regiment (Reserve of Officers), 3rd Bn. (Reserve); M.C.

Drewe, Rev. F. S., M.A., M.R.C.S., L.R.C.P. ... ... ... 1900-6 *b*
Medical Officer, Royal Air Force.

Druitt, Capt. G. T. ... ... 1905-10 *T.*
The Hampshire Regiment, 7th Bn. (T.); served in Egypt.

Druitt, Capt. J. V. ... ... 1901-5 *T.*
The Hampshire Regiment, 7th Bn. (T); served in Mesopotamia.

Drury, Lieut. P. H. ... ... 1910-13 *a*
The South Wales Borderers, 1st Bn.; attached R.A.F.

†Duckworth, 2nd Lieut. W. H. ... 1910-14 *a*
The Lancashire Fusiliers, 20th (S.) Bn.; died, April 14th, of wounds received in France, March 23rd, 1916.

Duke, Major A. B. C. ... ... 1902-6 *a*
R.F.A.; commanding 1093rd Battery, Lahore, India.

Duke, Capt. H. E. ... ... 1901-5 *a*
The Dorsetshire Regiment, 1/4th Bn. (T.)

DUMBLETON, Driver N. A. ... 1913-17 *T.*
Honourable Artillery Company.

DUNCAN, 2nd Lieut. D. C. ... 1901-2 *c*
The Royal Sussex Regiment, 3rd Bn. (Reserve).

DUNCAN, 2nd Lieut. J. A. ... 1903-4 *c*
The Royal Scots Fusiliers, 9th (S.) Bn.

*DUNCOMBE-ANDERSON, Capt. W.... 1885-89 *a*
Reserve of Officers, 1904, Gazetted to Cheshire Yeomanry, 1915; seconded for duty as temp. Major, Labour Corps, France, March, 1917, to March, 1919; twice mentioned in despatches; Military O.B.E.

*DUNKIN, Major H., T.D. ... 1893-*Master*
Unattached List (T.F.); O.C. Commanding Sherborne O.T.C., till January 1st, 1918; mentioned for War Service.

*DUNNING, Capt. B. R. ... ... 1907-11 *f*
The Devonshire Regiment, 10th (S.) Bn.; mentioned in despatches.

DUNSTON, Lieut. A. E. A. ... 1909-14 *a*
The King's Own (Royal Lancaster Regt.), 1st Bn. (transferred from The Dorsetshire Regiment, 2/4th Bn., T.); A.D.C., 1916; Flying Officer, 30th Squad. R.F.C. (Mil. Wing), 1916-1917; Political Dept., 1918.

DUSSEK, Capt. E. A. ... ... 1906-8 *d*
Royal Garrison Artillery.

†*DUVALL, Rev. (Capt.) J. R. ... 1902-6 *b*
Chaplain to 66th Brigade; attached to 13th Manchesters, 12th Cheshires, 7th Wilts; served in France, 1915; in Salonika, 1915-1917; died of wounds received in action, October 6th, 1917; mentioned in despatches.

Dyke, Lieut.-Col. O. M. ... 1893-6 *a*

Indian Army; 21st Prince Albert Victor's Own Cavalry (Frontier Force); Daly's Horse.

†Eagar, Lieut. D. G. ... ... 1912-17 *c*

Royal Field Artillery, B/160th Brigade; killed in action, on edge of Wytschaete Wood, September 28th, 1918.

†Eagar, Lieut. F. R. ... ... 1907-12 *c*

Royal Field Artillery, 8th Division, 30th Battery; killed at Fleurbaix, May 9th, 1915.

Eccles, Lance-Corpl. R. E. A. ... 1911-14 *f*

Honourable Artillery Company, 1st (Reserve) Bn.: discharged from Service, November 2nd, 1918.

Edlin, Lieut. P. A. M. ... 1911-14 *a*

The Royal Warwickshire Regiment, 2nd Bn.; wounded, May 4th, 1917, and October 13th, 1917.

†Edwards, Major B. ... ... 1897-9 *c*

Royal Garrison Artillery, Nigeria Regiment, 123rd Siege Battery; killed in France, March, 1917.

†*Egerton, 2nd Lieut. B. R. ... 1911-14 *c*

Royal Engineers, 87th Field Company; mentioned in despatches; killed at Lacelle, France, October 23rd, 1918.

Elderton, Capt. M. B. ... 1907-*Master*

Royal Garrison Artillery; served in France with 143rd Siege Battery, August, 1916, to June, 1917; and with 471st Siege Battery, May, 1918, to November, 1918.

Ellerton, Capt. W. M. ... 1882-3 *a*
H.M.S. Erin, (R.N.)

Elliott, Rev. E. A. ... ... 1904-8 *a*
Y.M.C.A.; served with 4th Army, B.E.F., France.

†Elliot, 2nd Lieut. W. E. ... 1906-9 *a*
The Dorsetshire Regiment, 7th (S.) Bn.; killed in France, September 26th, 1916.

†Elliott, 2nd Lieut. E. ... 1912-14 *g*
Royal Field Artillery; died of wounds received at Cambrai, October 8th, 1918.

†Ellis, Major C. A. ... ... 1885-8 *Price*
The Cameronians (Scottish Rifles), 2nd Bn.; killed in France at Neuve Chapelle, March 10th, 1915.

Ellis, Capt. G. R. ... 1899-1903 *a*
R.A.M.C.

†*Elsmie, Lieut.-Col. G. E. D. ... 1880-2 *a*
Commanding 20th Deccan Horse; killed in Mesopotamia; Officer Légion d'Honneur.

Elton, temp. Capt. H. B. 1894-1901 *a*
Royal Army Medical Corps; attached 10th (S.) Bn., Devonshire Regiment; served in France, September, 1915; Salonika, November, 1915, to August, 1916; invalided out, November 21st, 1916.

*English, Col. C. E. ... ... 1873-8 *a*
Royal Field Artillery; Reserve of Officers; mentioned in despatches (twice); O.B.E.

*ENSOR, Lieut.-Col. F. C. S. ... 1892-6 *a*
Army Ordnance Department; in Royal Garrison Artillery, Chief Ordnance Officer, Mauritius, until November, 1915; Officer i/c Ammunition, and later, Ordnance Officer, Base Depôt, Alexandria, from December 6th, 1915, to 1919; mentioned in despatches and for 'services in Mauritius'; Military O.B.E.

EVANS, 2nd Lieut. D. C. R. J. ... 1913-17 *a*
Royal Garrison Artillery.

EVANS, Midshipman R. ... 1910-13 *Prep.*
R.N.; December, 1916, H.M.S. Royal Sovereign.

EVAN-THOMAS, Lieut.-Col. A. ... 1858-62 *d*
7th Dragoon Guards.

*EVERINGTON, Major F. E. ... 1888-93 *f*
Royal Army Service Corps; mentioned in despatches.

FALCONER, Major E. A. ... ... 1894-7 *a*
Royal Air Force.

*FARRER, Major E. R. B. ... 1905-10 *a*
Royal Army Service Corps (Special Reserve; mentioned in despatches (twice); M.C.

FAWCETT, Lieut. C. H.... ... 1911-14 *d*
Royal Field Artillery, D/351 Battery; served with the 73rd Battery, 5th Brigade, R.F.A., Lahore Division, in France from September, 1916, to April, 1918; gassed at Loos, April 9th, 1918.

†FEARNLEY-WHITTINGSTALL, Lieut. G. H. ... ... ... 1907-9 *a*
(See 'WHITTINGSTALL').

*FENDALL, Col. (temp. Brig.-Gen.) C. P., D.S.O. ... ... ... 1874-7 *a*

Asst. Adjt. and Q.M.G., Administrative Staff, Dover Fortress; C.M.G., C.B.; mentioned in despatches (twice).

FENN, Col. E. H., C.I.E. ... 1861-5 *a*

Late R.A.M.C., Worcester Territorial Force Association; employed under the War Office for several months; resigned owing to ill-health; died, November 24th, 1916.

†FENN, Lieut. E. J. P. ... ... 1908-14 *a*

The Royal Welsh Fusiliers; attached to 1/5th Bn., The Essex Regiment; killed in action in Palestine, September 19th, 1918.

FINCH, Lieut. W. ... ... 1887-91 *a*

West Somerset Yeomanry (T.F.).

†FINDLAY, Capt. R. de C. ... 1883-7 *a*

Seaforth Highlanders (Ross-shire Buffs, The Duke of Albany's), 4th Bn.; killed at Neuve Chapelle, 11th March, 1915.

FIRTH, 2nd Lieut. J. E. A. ... 1912-17 *f*

Royal Garrison Artillery; 3rd (Reserve) Battery, R.H.A.

FISHER, Pte. H. W. T. ... 1911-13 *b*

Honourable Artillery Company; served with 2nd Bn., in France, 1916; wounded and invalided home, January, 1917; in France, December, 1917, to June, 1918; then with 1st (Reserve) Bn.

*FISHER, 2nd Lieut. R. ... ... 1916-17 *f*

R.N.V.R.; mentioned in despatches.

†Fitch, 2nd Lieut. D. ... ... 1911-13 *c*

Royal Field Artillery; served in France and Flanders from August 20th, 1916, until killed in the third battle of Ypres, October 16th, 1917.

Flack, 2nd Lieut. H. L. ... 1906-9 *c*

Royal Army Service Corps.

Flower, Lieut. E. J. ... ... 1910-14 *a*

R.F.A.; served in France; 1914-15 Star.

Flower, 2nd Lieut. W. M. ... 1911-14 *a*

5th Reserve Cavalry Regiment.

*Foley, Major W. B. ... ... 1903-7 *a*

R.A.M.C.; served in France; with Salonika Force from December, 1915, to November, 1918; with 28th C.C.S. during whole period; Surgical Specialist to unit from October, 1918; mentioned in despatches (twice); O.B.E.

†Folliott, 2nd Lieut. J. ... ... 1912-16 *c*

Durham Light Infantry; killed in France, September 19th, 1918.

Foot, Lieut. H. J. ... ... 1903-7 *T.*

The Welsh Regiment, 1/4th Bn. (T.); served in the Dardanelles with 53rd Division; severely wounded at Suvla Bay Landing, August 10th, 1915; subsequently Asst. Staff Officer at Headquarters, Pembroke Dock Garrison; then War Dept. Land Agent to the Western Command, Chester.

*Ford, Surgeon-Gen. R. W., D.S.O. 1874-5 *d*

Deputy Director of Medical Services in Egypt; K.C.M.G., C.B.

†FORREST, Lieut. E. A. A. ... 1904-10 *a*
The Gloucestershire Regiment, 11th (S.) Bn.; died of blood-poisoning at Malta, December 9th, 1915.

FORREST, Bombardier L. B. L. ... 1906-10 *a*
Australian Force; 5th Divisional Ammunition Column; served in France.

*FORSHAW, Capt. H. P. ... ... 1892-4 *a*
The King's Own (Royal Lancaster Regiment), 2/5th Bn. (T.); M.C.

FOSTER, 2nd Lieut. E. L. P. ... 1912-16 *a*
Indian Army, 39th Garhwal Rifles.

FOSTER, Capt. T. B. G. ... 1899-1903 *f*
The Cameronians (Scottish Rifles), 1st Bn.

FOX, 2nd Lieut. E. L. W. ... 1912-6 *b*
Indian Army, 39th Garhwal Rifles.

FOX, 2nd Lieut. R. de V. R. ... 1912-16 *g*
Indian Army, 45th Sikhs.

*FRASER, Major A. J. ... ... 1888-9 *b*
Royal Army Service Corps; Supply Depôts Northampton and Le Havre, August, 1914, to 1917; Assistant to D.A.D. of Supplies, H.Q., 2nd Army, France, April to November, 1917; Assistant to A.D. of Supplies, G.H.Q., Italy, November, 1917, to March, 1919; mentioned in despatches, December, 1917, and May, 1918; D.S.O. and La Croie al Merite di Guerra.

FRASER, Sergt. G. D. ... ... 1908-11 *b*
Canadian Expeditionary Force.

†FRASER, 2nd Lieut. V. A. D. ... 1914-17 *b*
Indian Army, 3rd (Q.V.O.) Corps of Guides; killed, November, 1919, in Expedition on N.W. Frontier.

*FREEMAN, Major C. T. ... ... 1908-11 *b*
Royal Air Force; D.S.O., A.F.C.

FREEMAN, 2nd Lieut. P. B. ... 1916-20 *Master*
Worcester Regt.; and Sherborne O.T.C.

FRENCH, Surgeon Lieut.-Comdr. A. G. V. ... ... 1896-1901 *a*
H.M.S. Vindex; 1914, was on H.M.S. Carnarvon in Falkland Islands action; 1917, was on H.M.S. Marshal Ney (Dover Patrol) in action with enemy destroyers; 1918, on H.M.S. Vindex in Eastern Mediterranean (anti-submarine work).

†FREUND, Corpl. E. W. T. ... 1909-14 *b*
Royal Engineers, 186th Company; died of wounds near Merville, December 22nd, 1915.

*FREWEN, Lieut.-Col. L. ... 1903-6 *f*
The King's Royal Rifle Corps, 8th (S.) Bn.; served in France, May, 1915 to January, 1917; invalided, May, 1917; mentioned in despatches (twice); D.S.O.

*FRINK, Capt. F. C. B. ... ... 1881-6 *b*
The South Staffordshire Regiment, 10th (S.) Bn.; attached Labour Corps; mentioned in despatches.

FRINK, 2nd Lieut. H. R. C. ... 1913-17 *b*
4th (Royal Irish) Dragoon Guards.

FRISBY, Lieut. N. ... ... 1909-13 *b*
The Duke of Edinburgh's (Wiltshire Regiment), 7th (S.) Bn.

†FROST, 2nd Lieut. A. C. ... 1911-14 *d*
Princess Louise's (Argyll and Sutherlandshire Highlanders), 11th (S.) Bn.; killed in France, September 27th, 1915.

FROST, 2nd Lieut. B. D. ... 1911-15 *b*

Essex Regiment; attached Royal Air Force.

†FROST, Lieut. J. J. ... ... 1910-14 *d*

The Northumberland Fusiliers, 11th (S.) Bn.; Senior Machine Gun Officer; killed in France, July 7th, 1916.

FUTCHER, 2nd Lieut. G. H. C. ... 1905-7 *c*

The Sherwood Foresters (Nottinghamshire and Derbyshire Regiment), 10th Bn.; from 1915 to 1917 a trooper in 1st King Edward's Horse, (The King's Oversea Dominions Regiment).

*GALLOWAY, Major (temp. Lieut.-Col.) A. G. ... ... ... 1892-4 *a*

Royal Army Service Corps; mentioned in despatches; D.S.O.

GARDNER-SMITH, Rev. P. ... 1902 *d*

Served in France with Church Army.

GARNIER, Lance-Corpl. The Rev. G. R. ... ... ... 1894-99 *a*

Enlisted in 1915 in M.T., A.S.C., saw service in France from August, 1916, to January, 1918, when discharged unfit.

GARSTIN, temp. Capt. C. F. ... 1894-7 *T.*

Chinese Labour Corps, 23rd Company.

GARSTIN, Major W. A. M. ... 1895-9 *T.*

Government of India Political Department.

*GATER, Major C. E. H. ... ... 1901-5 *a*

R.A.M.C.; Special Reserve; mentioned in despatches.

*GEE, Lieut.-Col. F. W., M.B. ... 1876-80 *d*
Indian Medical Service, attached to 5th Cavalry; mentioned in despatches (thrice); C.I.E.

GEIPEL, 2nd Lieut. L. H. H. ... 1905-7 *a*
Royal Field Artillery; 4th Northumbrian (Company of Durham) (Howitzer) Ammunition Column (T.).

†GERRARD, Capt. P. N. ... ... 1884-7 *d*
Malay States Volunteer Rifles; killed in the Singapore mutiny while Commandant, Prisoner of War Camp, Singapore, 1915.

GIBBONS, 2nd Lieut. H. ... 1912-15 *g*
Royal Military College, Sandhurst; 1st Bn. The Devonshire Regiment (attached 3rd Bn.).

†GIBBONS, 2nd Lieut. J. ... 1912-16 *g*
The Dorsetshire Regiment, 6th Bn.; died of wounds at Etaples, June 6th, 1917.

GIBBS, 2nd Lieut. A. R. ... 1899-1904 *a*
The Worcestershire Regiment, 7th Bn.; served in France; attached 13th Norfolks.

GIBBS, 2nd Lieut. C. B. ... 1905-9 *c*
The Duke of Edinburgh's (Wiltshire Regiment), 6th (S.) Bn.

GIBSON, Assist. Paymaster C. de V. 1906-9 *b*
H.M.S. 'Arrogant.'

*GIBSON, Capt. E. R. ... ... 1906-9 *d*
Royal Field Artillery; Staff Captain, R.A., 3rd Corps, B.E.F.; M.C.; mentioned in despatches (twice).

*Gibson Fleming, Capt. and Bt.-Major H. ... ... ... 1901-4 *c*

The Highland Light Infantry, 9th (Glasgow Highland) Bn. (T.); Assistant Director, Ministry of Munitions; mentioned in despatches.

Gilbert, Capt. R. F. E. ... 1885-7 *Price*

The Norfolk Regiment, 4th Bn. (T.).

Gill, Lieut.-Col. J. W. ... ... 1868-73 *a*

Royal Army Medical Corps.

*Glasgow, Bt. Lieut.-Col. (Hon. Brig. General) W. J. ... ... 1874-7 *c*

The Queen's (Royal West Surrey) Regiment; O.C. 7th Bn. in France; 50th Infantry Brigade and Tank Corps Training Centre (1917-18); mentioned in despatches; C.M.G.

Godfrey, 2nd Lieut. D. S. ... 1907-10 *b*

The Dorsetshire Regiment, 3rd Bn. (Reserve); attached 8th Bn., Devonshire Regiment.

†Goldsmith, Lieut. H. M. ... 1899-1904 *a*

The Devonshire Regiment, 3rd Bn.; Machine Gun Officer, 25th Brigade; killed near Fromelles, May 9th, 1915.

Goodrick, Gunner G. C. C. ... 1906-8 *a*

Royal Field Artillery, 187th Brigade.

Goodwyn, Cadet J. N. ... ... 1913-17 *b*

Household Brigade, Officer Cadet Bn.

GOODWYN, Capt. N. P. ... 1898-1900 *b*

The Worcestershire Regiment, 7th Bn.; relinquished commission on account of ill health, caused by wounds, with the honorary rank of Captain, February 14th, 1917.

*GORDON, Capt. C. A. ... 1897-1902 *T.*

Indian Army; 11th Rajputs (Duke of Connaught's Own); A.D.C., H.Q., 12th Brigade, I.E.F. 'D'; served in Mesopotamia; mentioned in despatches; M.C., D.S.O.

GORDON, Major G. S. ... ... 1893-8 *b*

Indian Army; 35th Scinde Horse.

GOSLING, Sergt. H. ... ... 1906-9 *a*

Honourable Artillery Company, 'B' Battery.

GOSSLING, 2nd Lieut. A. C. ... 1914-17 *c*

Royal Field Artillery.

GOULD, 2nd Lieut, G. ... ... 1914-17 *a*

Royal Air Force; served in France with 41st Kite Balloon Section, R.A.F.

*GOVER, Capt. A. C. ... ... 1898-1901 *a*

Indian Army, 121st Pioneers; M.C.

GRACE, Sub. Lieut. E. ... ... 1908-10 *Prep.*

1916, H.M.S. Australia.

GRAHAM, Paymaster Sub. Lieut. G. D. M. ... ... 1910-12 *d*

R.N.R., H.M.S. King George V.

GRAHAM-MONTGOMERY, Capt. G. J. E. ... ... ... 1908-11 *b*

The Hampshire Regiment, 12th (S.) Bn.

GRANGER-BROWNE, 2nd Lieut. H.F. 1913-16 *b*

The Devonshire Regiment, 16th Bn.

*GRANVILLE, Major C. (temp. Lieut.-Col.) ... ... 1886-9 *b*

The Devonshire Regiment, 3rd Bn., attached 1st Bn.; O.B.E.; mentioned in despatches.

*GRAVES, Capt. B. ... ... 1902-3 *a*

Served as Medical Officer to 5th and 6th Bns., The Prince of Wales's (North Staffordshire Regiment) and to 10th and 13th Bns., The Royal Fusiliers (City of London Regiment), in France, and to 19th Brigade, Royal Field Artillery, in Salonika; Opthalmic Surgeon in charge of 56th and 82nd Army Opthalmic Centres from Armistice till demobilization; M.C.

†GRAY, 2nd Lieut. G. E. M. ... 1908-12 *f*

The Northumberland Fusiliers, 14th (S.) Bn.; killed, July 14th, 1916, at Bazentin le petit.

†GRAY, Capt. H. M. ... ... 1908-10 *f*

The Royal Fusiliers (City of London Regiment), 11th Bn.; severely wounded in attack on Thiepval, 1916; wounded and missing (since assumed killed), August 10th, 1917, in Ypres—Menin Road battle.

GREATHEAD, Lieut. A. M. ... 1901-1904 *c*

Royal Engineers, 56th Field Company.

*GREATHEAD, a./Major J. M. ... 1901-3 *c*
Royal Engineers; mentioned in despatches; M.C.

GREENHILL, Capt. H. M. ... 1898-1900 *b*
The Dorsetshire Regiment, 3rd Bn. (Reserve).

GREENSLADE, Lieut. R. S. ... 1909-11 *d*
Somerset Royal Horse Artillery; Motor Machine Gun Service; 100th Squadron, R.A.F.; served in France; prisoner of War in Germany for 14 months.

*GREENSTREET, Bt. Lieut.-Col. C. B. L. ... ... ... 1885-8 *a*
Royal Engineers; mentioned in despatches (four times, for work in Mesopotamia); Serbian Order of the White Eagle, 4th Class with Swords.

*GREGORIE, Bt. Lieut.-Col. H. G. 1893-7 *a*
The Royal Irish Regiment, 2nd Bn.; mentioned in despatches (thrice); Légion d' Honneur, Croix d' Officier; D.S.O.

GREGORY, 2nd Lieut. C. A. ... 1912-16 *c*
The Essex Regiment.

*GREVILLE, Capt. a./Lieut.-Col. G. G. F. F. ... ... 1899-1901 *a*
The Prince of Wales's Leinster Regiment (Royal Canadians), 1st Bn.; mentioned in despatches.

GREVILLE-HARSTON, Brig.-Gen. C. 1860-4 *T.*
Chief Inspector of Arms and Ammunition, Canadian Expeditionary Forces Headquarters Staffs; served in France.

†GRIERSON, Lieut. S. D. ... ... 1912-17 *f*

Seaforth Highlanders (Ross-shire Buffs, The Duke of Albany's); killed in France, August 30th, 1918.

*GRIFFIN, Major (a./Lieut.-Col.) J. A. A. ... ... ... 1905-8 *a*

The Lincolnshire Regiment, 2nd Bn.; April and May, 1918, a./Lieut.-Col., commanding 2nd Bn., Princess Charlotte of Wales's (Royal Berkshire Regiment); mentioned in despatches (twice); D.S.O.

GRIMLEY, 2nd Lieut. A. T. ... 1912-16 *c*

The Dorsetshire Regiment, 3rd Bn.

GROVE, Lieut. G. ... ... 1902-6 *f*

King's African Rifles; temp. A.D.C. to Lord Buxton.

†GROVE, 2nd Lieut. (a./Capt. and Adjt.) P. C. ... ... ... 1911-15 *f*

Seaforth Highlanders (Ross-shire Buffs, The Duke of Albany's), 2nd Bn.; killed at the battle of Arras, April 11th, 1917.

†GROVES, Corpl. J. S. ... ... 1908-10 *a*

30th British Columbia Horse, attached 3rd Canadian Signal Corps as a Motor Despatch Rider; died near Hazebrouck, France, January 17th, after an accident on the night of January 15th, 1916, whilst carrying a message.

†GROVES, Lance-Corpl. R. E. ... 1910-11 *a*

11th Canadian Mounted Rifles; killed in action, March 27th, 1917.

GUIMARAENS, Paul ... ... 1910-14 *Prep.*
R.N.; 1917, H.M.S. Alsatian (10th Cruiser Squadron).

*GULLICK, Capt. C. D. ... ... 1906-11 *d*
The Buffs (East Kent Regiment), 6th (S.) Bn.; M.C. and bar.

†GUNNING, Lieut. J. W. ... ... 1911-14 *g*
The Duke of Edinburgh's (Wiltshire Regiment), 1st Bn.; killed at the battle of Bapaume, March 21st, 1918.

GUPPY, 2nd Lieut. R. ... ... 1907-8 *b*
The Dorsetshire Regt, 3rd Bn. (Reserve).

*GURNEY, Capt. J. C. ... ... 1906-12 *f*
The Northamptonshire Regiment, 7th (S.) Bn.; G.S.O., 3rd Grade, 2nd Army Headquarters; mentioned in despatches (twice); Belgian Croix de Guerre; O.B.E.

GWYTHER, Major E. J. ... ... 1888-91 *T.*
Leicester Regiment, attached 273rd Infantry Bn.; gassed in Mametz Wood.

†GWYTHER, Corpl. P. H. ... ... 1892-3 *a*
South Staffordshire Regiment; killed at Ypres, January 12th, 1917.

*HAES, a./Capt. C. P. M. ... 1890-3 *u*
Royal Army Service Corps; served in France; Officer Order de L'Etoile Noire.

*HALL, Major (temp. Lieut.-Col.) E.G. 1897-9 *d*

117th Mahrattas; D.A. Q.-M.-G., Headquarters Staff, Simla; served in the 6th (Poona) Division, Mesopotamia; wounded at Zaim, November 17th, 1914, and at Ctesiphon, November 22nd, 1915; mentioned in despatches (thrice); Order of Kara George, 4th Class, with swords; C.I.E.

†HALLIDAY, 2nd Lieut. C. G. R. ... 1911-14 *g*

Royal Engineers; entered Woolwich, December, 1914; transferred to Chatham, July, 1915; went to France, February, 1916, to 1st Field Squadron, R.E., attached to 1st Cavalry Division; was transferred to 225th Field Co., R.E., on June 1st, 1917. Killed at Ypres on June 13th, 1917.

HALLIDAY, Lieut. G. R.... ... 1909-10 *b*

Royal Garrison Artillery; No. 1 Battery; No. 3 Siege (Reserve) Brigade; served in India, January, 1915, to January, 1917, with 1st Wessex Brigade, R.F.A. (T.), and then in Mesopotamia with 74th Brigade, Heavy Artillery, until December, 1918.

HAMILTON, Lieut. C. F. H. ... 1911-16 *d*

Royal Field Artillery; served in France from January 3rd, 1917, till wounded on March 25th, 1918.

HAMLING, Lieut. H. H.... ... 1902-4 *c*

King's African Rifles, 3rd Bn.; served 15 months as private in 2nd Rhodesian Regiment.

HAMMOND, W. C. W. ... ... 1911-12 *g*

American Protective League (Secret Service), also British Recruiting Mission, Chicago.

HAMMOND, Major W. P. ... 1897-1900 *a*

Indian Army, 18th Infantry.

HAMPTON, Capt. R. W. ... ... 1904-8 *f*

The Royal Fusiliers (City of London Regiment), 8th (S.) Bn.; attached 5th Bn.; on Staff, Embarkation, Tilbury Docks.

†HAMPTON, Rifleman W. ... ... 1905-9 *f*

The London Regiment; joined 1st Bn. London Rifle Brigade, in August, 1914; went to France, November 7th, 1914; shot in the neck by a sniper, January 16th, 1915, whilst wiring, and died May 14th, 1915, at a nursing home in London.

HANKEY, Major C. A. A. ... 1882-6 *a*

The Highland Light Infantry, 14th (S.) Bn.; Assistant Provost Marshal, Winchester.

*HANKEY, Major (temp. Col.) S. R. A. 1888-92 *a*

(Ret.), South Irish Horse (late 3rd Dragoon Guards), Dep. Director of Remounts, 3rd Army, B.E.F.; Special Reserve; South Irish Horse; mentioned in despatches; D.S.O.

HARDY, Capt. H. de L. ... ... 1908-12 *c*

Indian Police, and Indian Army Reserve of Officers; died at Denapur, after a short illness, on August 30th, 1919.

HARE, Lieut. P. V. ... ... 1913-15 *c*

The Artists Rifles; 8th Bn. Sherwood Foresters; 7th Bn. Gloucester Regiment; and 270th Company Machine Gun Corps.

HARRIS, Pte. J. B. ... ... 1899-1904 *b*

Canadian Infantry, 188th Bn.; and Canadian Flying Corps.

*HARRIS, 2nd Lieut. M. W. S. ... 1911-14 *g*

The Duke of Cambridge's Own (Middlesex Regiment), 4th Bn.; M.C.

HARRIS, Cadet R. L. A.... ... 1913-18 *f*

R.E. Cadet School.

HARRIS, Midshipman R. R. ... 1914-15 *g*

H.M.S. Iron Duke.

HARRIS, Capt. W. J., M.D., F.R.C.P. 1880-4 *f*

R.A.M.C. (T.F.); Neurologist, 3rd London General Hospital.

HARRISON, Lieut.-Col. H. ... 1883-9 *a*

Indian Political Department.

HARSTON, 2nd Lieut. W. W. ... 1913-17 *a*

The Dorsetshire Regiment, 3rd Bn.

HART, Pte. G. ... ... ... 1915-17 *b*

Inns of Court O.T.C.; 3rd Bn. London Scottish; 51st Bn. Gordon Highlanders; served in France.

HARVEY, Lieut. C. D. W. ... 1908-11 *T.*

The Dorsetshire Regiment, 7th (S.) Bn.; later attached to 1/6th Gurkhas, Abbotabad; wounded on the Somme, 1916, and at Cambrai, June, 1918.

HARVEY, Lieut. R. W. ... ... 1912-13 *T.*

The Dorsetshire Regiment, 3rd Bn. (Reserve); attached 6th Bn. in France; also to Royal Air Force (Observer), 42nd Squadron.

HASLER, Lieut. F. G. ... ... 1912-15 *g*

Royal Field Artillery; served in France, October, 1917, to February, 1918, with C/177th Brigade, R.F.A., 16th (Irish) Division; invalided out, 1919.

*HATTON-HALL, Capt. H. C. ... 1907-9 *c*

The King's Own Scottish Borderers; attached to Machine Gun Corps and subsequently to Tank Corps; M.C.

*HAWKEY-SHEPHERD, Major J. G. 1899-1902 *f*

County of London Yeomanry, 2nd Coy. (Westminster Dragoons), T.F.; mentioned in despatches; M.C.

HAWKINS, 2nd Lieut. C. L. M. ... 1913-17 *a*

Dorsetshire Regiment, 3rd Bn.; served previously in Inns of Court O.T.C. and 20th Officer Cadet Bn.

*HAWLEY-EDWARDS, Lieut. S. F. 1895-1900 *a*

Mentioned in despatches.

†*HAY, Capt. G. W. ... ... 1893-6 *a*

The Loyal North Lancashire Regiment, 3rd Bn. (Reserve); August, 1914, placed on Coast defence at Felixtowe; December, 1914, joined 1st Bn. L. N. Lancs. in France; December 21st, 1914, slightly wounded at Festubert; May 9th, 1915, killed in action at Richebourg l'Avonée; mentioned in despatches.

*HAY, Mr. K. R. ... ... 1887-91 *a*

Civilian M.O., 1st London General Hospital; rejected for general service; O.B.E.

HAYNES, Pte. S. H. ... ... 1901-5 *d*

The London Regiment, 28th (County of London) Bn. (Artists' Rifles) (T.F.); invalided out.

HAYTER, 2nd Lieut. E. G. E. ... 1908-10 *a*

Royal Field Artillery, 68th Brigade, 17th Division; served in Egypt; with 11th Division, in Gallipoli, 1915; with 10th Division in 1st Serbian campaign, 1915-16; in France, 1917; gassed and invalided home; in Palestine, 1918.

HAYTER, Lieut. F. C. E. ... 1914-16 *a*

Royal Air Force, 16th Squadron; served in France, June, 1918; worked for 18th Corps and then for 8th.

HAYTER, Lieut. G. R. E. ... 1910-13 *a*

Royal Air Force, 12th Squadron; served in France; previously in the Hampshire Regiment, 9th (Cyclist) Bn. (T.).

HAYTER, 2nd Lieut. T. J. ... 1901-3 *a*

The Loyal North Lancashire Regiment, 7th (S.) Bn.; attached 6th (S.) Bn. (38th Brigade, 13th Division); served in Gallipoli till evacuation, November, 1915; discharged owing to ill-health.

*HEMPSON, Capt. G. O. ... ... 1903-7 *a*

R.A.M.C.; served in France and Cyprus; mentioned in despatches.

HEMPSON, 2nd Lieut. V. A. ... 1900-4 *a*

Royal Field Artillery; badly gassed in France, 1917.

*HENDERSON, Lieut. E. C. ... 1902-5 *b*

The Northumberland Fusiliers, 6th Bn.; attached 21st Bn.; severely wounded at Greenland Hill, Arras, June 5th, 1917; M.C.

*HENNIKER-GOTLEY, Major G. R. ... 1908-11 *c*

The Prince of Wales's (North Staffordshire Regt.); 91st Coy., Machine Gun Corps; mentioned in despatches (thrice); D.S.O.

*HENRI, Major P. R. ... ... 1905-9 *c*

The Royal Fusiliers (City of London Regiment), 1/3rd Bn.; D.S.O.; M.C. and bar; Croix de Guerre.

HERBAGE, Lieut. K. A. ... ... 1912-13 *c*

Royal Field Artillery; served in France and with the North Russia Relief Force; gassed.

†HERBAGE, Pte. S. H. W. ... 1910-13 *c*

The London Regiment, 1st Bn., London Rifle Brigade; went to France, November 4th, 1914, and was killed in action, January 20th, 1915.

*HERBERT, Major D. M. A. ... 1910-14 *c*

Indian Army; 82nd Punjabis; served in Mesopotamia; mentioned in despatches; M.C.

HERIZ-SMITH, 2nd Lieut. The Rev. E. E. A. ... ... ... 1912-17 ***Master***

Unattached List (T.F.); Sherborne O.T.C.

*HESSE, Major J. H. B. ... ... 1886-90 *Price*

Royal Army Service Corps; Mechanical Transport; served in France; mentioned in despatches.

*HEXT, 2nd Lieut. A. C. ... ... 1908-12 *a*

2nd East Riding of Yorkshire Yeomanry (T.F.); M.B.E.

HEXT, Lieut.-Col. F. M. ... 1875-8 *a*

The Devonshire Regiment, 10th (S.) Bn.; served in France, 1915; Macedonia, 1916; gazetted command The Sherwood Foresters (Nottinghamshire and Derbyshire Regt.), July 25th, 1916 (at Home); employed under War Office (M.I. 8 branch), 1917 and 1918.

*HEXT, Capt. (temp. Major) G. T. B. 1894-8 *c*

Indian Army; served in British East Africa; D.S.O.

*HEYWOOD, Lieut.-Col. Sir G.P., Bart. 1893-7 *a*

Yeomanry, Territorial Force; Staffordshire (Queen's Own Royal Regt.); served with the Egyptian Expeditionary Force, 1915-18; mentioned in despatches; D.S.O.

†HICKS, Col. F. R. ... ... 1882-9 *a*

The Hampshire Regiment; August 22nd, 1914, went to France, 2nd in Command of 1st Bn., and was wounded at LeCateau. November, 1914, returned to France in Command of 1st Bn.; May 8th, 1915, again wounded, at La Brique, near Ypres, and died at Guy's Hospital on June 12th, 1915.

HINDLE, 2nd Lieut. M. D. ... 1914-17

Indian Army; 2/35th Sikhs.

*HITCH, Lieut.-Col. A. T. ... 1907-11 *b*

The Lincolnshire Regiment; a./Lieut.-Col. in command 8th (S.) Bn.; served with 6th (S.) Bn., and 3rd (Reserve) Bn., The Bedfordshire Regt.; 2nd in command 11th (S.) Bn., The Royal Warwickshire Regt., November and December, 1917; wounded, February 12th, 1916; mentioned in despatches; D.S.O.

HITCHCOCK, Capt. R. V. ... 1898-1902 *f*

Royal Engineers.

HITCHINGS, Lieut N. J. ... ... 1884-7 *d*

East African Transport Corps.

HOBSON, Capt. E. R. C. ... 1910-13 *a*

British West Indies Regiment; attached Z Squadron, Royal Air Force.

HODDER, Bt. Col. W. M. ... 1874-7 *c*

Royal Engineers (Reserve of Officers).

*HODGES, Capt. A. P. ... ... 1910-12 *c*

Royal Field Artillery; 2nd Lieut., July 17th, 1914; France and Belgium, 1914-1918; Siberia, 1919; promoted Lieut. June 9th, 1915; a./Capt., August 25th, 1916; a./Major, September 25th, 1916; Capt., November 3rd, 1917; Military Cross, January 1st, 1918; severely wounded, March 21st, 1918; mentioned in despatches, January 1st, 1919.

†HODGES, 2nd Lieut. H. B. ... 1910-14 *b*

The King's Own (Yorkshire Light Infantry), 2nd Bn.; August, 1914, entered Sandhurst; December 23rd, 1914, gazetted 2nd Lieut.; March, 1915, went to France; April 18th, 1915, killed at Hill 60, near Ypres.

*HODGES, Capt. J. F. ... ... 1902-6 *a*
Princess Victoria's (Royal Irish Fusiliers), 2nd Bn.; mentioned in despatches; M.C. and bar.

HODGSON, 2nd Lieut. E. ... ... 1918-*Master*
Unattached List (T.F.); Sherborne School O.T.C.

†HODGSON, Lieut. R. E. ... ... 1908-13 *a*
The King's (Liverpool Regiment), 4th Bn.; attached R.A.F.; Pilot, July, 1918; killed in Belgium, while flying over the German trenches, September, 15th, 1918.

*HODSDON, Major J. W. B., M.D., F.R.C.S. ... ... ... 1872-5 *b*
R.A.M.C. (T.F.); 2nd Scottish General Hospital; O.B.E. (Military); mentioned for War Services.

HOGG, Capt. A. R. ... ... 1910-14 *a*
The Queen's Own (Royal West Kent Regiment), 7th (S.) Bn.; served in France, December 8th, 1915, till October 26th, 1917; then wounded (second time) and had foot amputated.

HOLDEN, Lieut. (temp. Capt.) E. G. 1909-14 *a*
Princess Charlotte of Wales's (Royal Berkshire Regiment); attached 139th Bn., Machine Gun Corps.

*HOLDEN, Capt. G. H. R., M.A., M.D., B.C. (Cantab.), M.R.C.S. (Eng.), L.R.C.P. (London) ... ... ... 1877-82 *a*
R.A.M.C. (T.F.); 3rd General Hospital, Oxford; seconded for Service at Reading War Hospital, March, 1915, Officer in Charge of Officers' Section; mentioned for War Services.

HOLDEN, a./Corpl. R. W. ... 1914-18 *a*
Inns of Court O.T.C. and 2nd Bn., King's Royal Rifle Corps.

†HOLMES, 2nd Lieut. B. R. G. ... 1908-12 *b*
Royal Field Artillery, 3/4th Northumbrian (Co. of Durham) (Howitzer) Brigade (T.); Commissioned, July, 1915; joined London Anti Aircraft defences, and was in charge of a Station; killed in action, in France, October 1st, 1917.

HOLMES, Lieut. B. S. (see Scott-Holmes)

*HOLMES, Major P. L. ... ... 1903-7 *b*
R.N.A.S.; D.S.C.; mentioned in despatches.

HOLT, Lieut. G. F. ... ... 1882-6 *b*
Royal Army Medical Corps.

HOMFRAY, Lieut. H. C. R. ... 1905-8 *f*
2nd Glamorgan Yeomanry (T.F.); retired on account of ill-health, March 1st, 1917.

HOMFRAY, Pte. K. ... ... 1910-12 *a*
Royal Army Service Corps (M.T.); served with Mesopotamian Expeditionary Force.

HOMFRAY, Capt. R. ... ... 1905-10 *a*
The Worcestershire Regiment, 1/7th Bn.; served with Italian Expeditionary Force.

HONNYWILL, Capt. G. W. ... 1889-95 *a*
Royal Army Service Corps.

*HOOPER, Capt. A. W. ... ... 1904-8 *a*
Royal Garrison Artillery, Forth R.G.A. (T.); 152nd Siege Battery; M.C.

Hooper, Lieut. C. J. ... ... 1911-14 *d*
The Dorsetshire Regiment, 4th (Reserve) Bn.; served in France.

*Hooper, Capt. D. S. ... ... 1902-6 *a*
The Dorsetshire Regiment, 3rd (Reserve) Bn.; The Tank Corps; wounded, July, 1916; mentioned in despatches; M.C.

†Hooper, 2nd Lieut. L. J. ... 1908-13 *a*
The Dorsetshire Regiment, 7th (S.) Bn., attached 5th Bn.; served in Gallipoli; killed on September 26th, 1916, near Mouquet Farm, on the Somme.

Hooper, Corpl. M. ... ... 1906-10 *d*
Dorset Yeomanry (Queen's Own), 1st Bn.; served in Egypt; wounded.

Hope, Major L. C. ... ... 1886-9 *f*
The Dorsetshire Regiment, 2nd Bn.

Hope, Sergt. P. P. ... ... 1905-6 *T.*
Royal Engineers, Motor Cycle Despatch Rider.

Horne, Lieut. G. S. ... ... 1902-5 *f*
The Royal Fusiliers (City of London Regiment), 3/4th Bn.

*Hornidge, Capt. E. S. ... ... 1901-6 *c*
Royal Army Service Corps; mentioned in despatches; O.B.E.

Hornidge, 2nd Lieut. M. S. ... 1913-16 *c*
North Irish Horse.

HORSFALL, Lieut. T. M. ... 1897-1902 *a*

Royal Army Service Corps (H.T.), late Border Regt.; served in France, Salonika, Bulgaria, Constantinople, Turkey in Asia, The Caucasus; invalided home from Russia, in 1919.

HORTON, Sub-Lieut. A. ... ... 1911-13 *Prep.*

Royal Navy; 1917, H.M.S. Agincourt; 1918, H.M.S. Orion.

†HOSKINS, 2nd Lieut. F. D. ... 1910-14 *d*

The Prince of Wales's (North Staffordshire Regt.), 1st Bn.; August, 1914, entered Sandhurst; December 10th, 1914, gazetted 2nd Lieut., N. Staffs. Regt.; March, 1915, went to France to 1st Bn. at Ypres; July, 1915, appointed Bn. M.G. Officer; October 2nd, 1915, died from Shell Splinter wound in the head received previous day.

HOSKINS, Lieut. N. M. ... ... 1908-11 *d*

Enlisted in The London Regiment, 1/14th (County of London) Bn. (London Scottish), attached to 3/14th Bn. Commissioned to Balloon Section, R.A.F.

*HOVIL, Major R. ... ... 1894-6 *d*

Royal Field Artillery, 'A' Battery, 75th Brigade; served in France, with Guards' Division; mentioned in despatches; D.S.O.

HOW, Lieut.-Col. A. P. ... ... 1881-5 *a*

Indian Army, 114th Mahrattas; 2nd in Command.

HOW, Capt. D. ... ... ... 1888-92 *a*

The Welsh Regiment, 20th (S.) Bn. (3rd Rhondda) (late 3rd Bn., Reserve).

HOWARD-SMITH, Cadet J. ... 1914-18 *c*
Royal Field Artillery; 212th Battery, 2 B. Brigade.

HOWELL, 2nd Lieut. H. L. ... 1913-17 *d*
Royal Garrison Artillery.

HOWSE, 2nd Lieut. E. C. ... 1914-18 *d*
Loyal North Lancashire Regiment, 1st Bn.; previously R.M. College, Sandhurst.

*HUDSON, Capt. (temp. Lieut.-Col.) and Bt. Major C. E. ... ... 1905-10 *c*
The Sherwood Foresters (Nottinghamshire and Derbyshire Regiment), 2nd Bn.; mentioned in despatches (5 times); V.C.; D.S.O.; M.C.; Croix de Guerre; Italian silver medal for valour.

HUDSON, Capt. T. H. ... ... 1903-6 *c*
The Sherwood Foresters (Nottinghamshire and Derbyshire Regt.), 2/4th Bn. (extra Reserve), attached 2nd Bn.

HUGHES, Lieut. H. C. ... ... 1907-11 *b*
Royal Field Artillery, 2/3rd Hampsnire Battery, 1st Wessex Brigade (T.); served in India, January 7th, 1915, to September 16th, 1916; then in Mesopotamia, with 56th Brigade, R.F.A., until December 31st, 1917; and in France until wounded, August 26th, 1918; demobilized, January 27th, 1919.

*HULBERT, Major T. E. ... ... 1895-7 *f*
Indian Army, 3rd Skinner's Horse; served in France, November, 1914, to August, 1916; attached to 10th Lancers in Mesopotamia, November, 1916, to July, 1917; appointed Commandant, Branch School of Musketry, Satara, October, 1917; mentioned in despatches.

*HUNNYBUN, Major K. ... ... 1901-6 *f*

The Huntingdonshire Cyclist Battalion; attached 7th Bn., Prince Albert's (Somerset Light Infantry; mentioned in despatches; D.S.O.

HUNT, Lieut. E. G. ... ... 1895-99 *a*

(late Capt., unattached List, T.F.); Royal Welsh Fusiliers, 3rd (Reserve) Garrison Bn.; September, 1917, Gas Officer, attached R.A.M.C. Depôt, Blackpool.

HUNT, 2nd Lieut. W. H. ... 1912-16 *g*

Royal Garrison Artillery.

HUNTER, Capt. P. D. ... ... 1887-92 *c*

Royal Army Medical Corps; Neurologist, Gateshead War Hospital.

†HYLAND, 2nd Lieut. H. B. ... 1910-11 *c*

Enlisted in East Kent Yeomanry, September, 1914; transferred to 20th (S.) Bn. (3rd Rhondda), The Welsh Regiment, in Spring, 1915, and was Commissioned there in Autumn, 1915; transferred to 100th Coy., Machine Gun Corps; went to France, March, 1916; killed in action at High Wood, Battle of the Somme, 18th July, 1916.

ILLINGWORTH, Sub-Lieut. H. A. ... 1913-17 *a*

R.N.V.R.

*IREMONGER, Col. E. A. ... ... 1878-81 *f*

(late Durham Light Infantry); The Depôt, The Queen's Own (Royal West Kent Regt.); mentioned for War Services; G.B.E.

IREMONGER, Lieut.-Col. R. G. ... 1869-72 *f*

(Ret. Indian Army), Staff-Capt., G.S.O., 3rd Grade.

JACKMAN, Sub-Lieut. W. F. ... 1909-11 *c*
R.N.R., H.M.S. Goshawk.

†JACKSON-TAYLOR, 2nd Lieut. J. C. 1912-16 *c*
The King's Shropshire Light Infantry, 1st Bn. (Commissioned from Sandhurst); killed at Cambrai, France, March 21st, 1918.

JACKSON-TAYLOR, Major P. S. ... 1909-14 *c*
The Herefordshire Regiment, 1st Bn.; obtained Commission in 1914; went to Gallipoli, 1915, and was there till wounded, November, 1915; joined Royal Flying Corps, January, 1916, and went to France in summer of 1917, rising to be Major (now Capt., R.F.C., Regular Army).

*JACOB, Lieut.-Col. A. L., C.I.E. ... 1886-9 *a*
Indian Army (Political Department); O.B.E.

*JACOB, Brig.-Gen. A. le G., C.I.E., D.S.O. ... ... ... 1877-84 *a*
Commandant 106th Hazara Pioneers; G.S.O., 1/4th (Quetta Division); A.A. D. Q.M.G., Base Headquarters, Mesopotamia Expeditionary Force; A.D.C. to H.M. the King; mentioned in despatches; C.M.G.

*JACOB, Lieut.-Gen. Sir C. W. ... 1875-81 *a*
G.O.C., 2nd Army Corps, B.E.F., from May 28th, 1916; previously commanded Dehra Dun Brigade, January to September, 1915; Meerut Division to November, 1915; 21st Division to May, 1916; mentioned in despatches (nine times); C.B.; K.C.B.; K.C.M.G.; C.M.G.; Commandant Légion d'Honneur; Croix de Guerre; Grand Officier, Ordre de la Couronne; Grand

Officier, Order de Leopold avec Croix de Guerre (Belgian); Grand Officier, Légion d'Honneur (French); Distinguished Conduct Medal (America).

*JAMES, Bt. Lieut.-Col. A. H. C. ... 1887-90 *Price*
The South Staffordshire Regiment, 1st Bn.; Asst. Provost Marshal, 3rd Corps, August, 1914, to October, 1915; then Provost Marshal, 3rd Army, to August 4th, 1918; then Provost Marshal Forces in Great Britain, with rank of temp. Brig.-Gen.; wounded, October, 1914; mentioned in despatches (four times); Officier de la Légion d'Honneur; M.V.O.; D.S.O.

JAMES, 2nd Lieut. C. J. B. (formerly Scholey) ... ... ... 1912-17 *a*
London Regiment, 12th (County of London) Bn. (The Rangers).

JAMES, C. N. ... ... ... 1901-5 *a*
Indian Police; District Superintendant of Police, 4th Grade.

†JANASZ, 2nd Lieut. J. G. G. ... 1907-12 *b*
The Dorsetshire Regiment; gazetted to 3rd Bn. (Reserve), November 4th, 1914; sent to France and attached 2nd Bn., Wiltshire Regt., in March, 1915; killed, near Festubert, June 15th, 1915.

JEFFERSON, Asst. Paymaster E.A.R. 1910-14 *f*
Served on H.M.H.S. Mauretania, and H.M. Transports, Andania, Carpathia and Czaritza; attached to Naval Transport Service (Mercantile Marine).

JEFFREYS, 2nd Lieut. R. H. ... 1910-11 *c*
The Welsh Regiment, 20th (S.) Bn. (3rd Rhondda); resigned, 1917, on account of ill-health.

†JEFFREYS, Lieut. W. S. ... ... 1911-14 *c*
The Welsh Regiment, 13th (S.) Bn. (2nd Rhondda); served in France, 1915-16; reported wounded and missing, in Mametz Wood, July 9th, 1916; later reported killed.

†JENKINS, Lieut. R. B. ... ... 1910-14 *b*
The South Wales Borderers; gazetted to 5th (S.) Bn., September 19th, 1914; entered Sandhurst, December 31st, 1914; gazetted to 2nd Bn., S. W. Borderers, attached R.F.C., on June 16th, 1915; gazetted Flying Officer, September, 1915; joined No. 9 Squadron, in France, December 19th, 1915; died of wounds in France, January 17th, 1916, received in fight with a Fokker plane.

JENKINSON, Lance-Sergt. E. A. ... 1907-8 *d*
The Royal Fusiliers (City of London Regiment), 28th Bn. (Reserve).

JENNINGS, Lieut. G. W. ... ... 1901-4 *a*
Royal Field Artillery; attached G.H.Q., the Forces in Great Britain, June, 1917, to August, 1918; temp. Secretary, British Embassy, Madrid, September, 1918, to April, 1919.

*JEPHSON, Lieut. J. H. ... ... 1911-14 *a*
Royal Garrison Artillery, 2/No. 2 Company, Lewes, Sussex; and 24th Squadron R.A.F.; mentioned for War Services.

†*JESSON, Major R. W. F. ... 1901-5 *d*
The Duke of Edinburgh's (Wiltshire Regiment); joined as 2nd Lieut., 5th (S.) Bn., in August, 1914; wounded in Gallipoli; mentioned in despatches; killed, while 2nd in Command of Regt., near Kut, February 22nd, 1917.

*JOHNSON, Lieut.-Col. W. R. ... 1902-5 *a*
The Essex Regiment, 1/7th Bn. (T.); mentioned in despatches (twice); D.S.O.;C.B.E.

*JOHNSTON, Bt. Major D. S. ... 1900-4 *a*
Royal Engineers; mentioned in despatches.

JOHNSTONE, Lieut. C. A. ... 1901-3 *a*
The Dorsetshire Regiment, 6th Bn.; served in France; Liaison Officer with Portugese Corps; joined 3rd Bn., Rifle Brigade.

JOHNSTONE, Lieut. C. R. ... 1894-7 *d*
The Dorsetshire Regiment, 7th (S.) Bn.; Transport Officer.

JOHNSTONE, Capt. M. B. S. ... 1906-9 *f*
Army Remount Service; served in Salonika; commanding 49th Remount Squadron, 1918.

*JONES, Capt. H. E. ... ... 1894-7 *a*
Royal Sussex Regiment, 13th (S.) Bn.; gazetted 2nd Lieut., September, 1915; served in France from March, 1916, to October, 1918; a./Capt. and a./Staff-Capt., 116th Infantry Brigade; wounded, September, 1918; on the Wytschaete Ridge; mentioned in despatches (twice); M.C.

JONES-EVANS, Sub-Lieut. E. J. L. 1913-15 *c*
R.N.V.R.; served on H.M.S. Lookout and H.M.S. Porpoise.

JUDKINS, 2nd Lieut. B. E. H. ... 1898-1901 *a*
13th Hussars (serving with 12th Reserve Regiment of Cavalry).

*KEIR, Surgeon Comdr. W. W. ... 1891-3 *a*

Royal Navy; mentioned in despatches; C.M.G.; Légion d'Honneur (Chevalier).

KELLY, Capt. B. J. R. ... ... 1906-10 *a*

The South Wales Borderers, 3rd Bn. (Reserve).

*KEMP, Major F. W. ... ... 1893-9 *a*

New Zealand Medical Corps; D.A.D.M.S., N.Z. Division (October, 1918); M.C.

KENDLE, Major F. C. ... ... 1890 *Price*

Royal Marine Artillery; Instructor of Gunnery, Eastney Barracks, Portsmouth; served on H.M.S. Agincourt, August 8th, 1914, to July 25th, 1915.

KENDLE, Capt. G. H. ... ... 1900-2 *c*

Royal Marine Artillery; H.M.S. Monarch.

†*KENDLE, Major R. H. ... ... 1890 *Price*

The Suffolk Regiment, 5th Bn. (T.); as Hon. Capt. in Regulars, volunteered for foreign service; 1915, gazetted Major, made a district Musketry Instructor, and received Volunteer Decoration; went to Gallipoli, July, 1915; killed in a bayonet charge at Sulva Bay, August 12th, 1915.

†*KESTELL-CORNISH, Capt. R. V. ... 1908-14 *a*

Gazetted The Dorsetshire Regt., 1st Bn., August, 1914; Adjutant, November, 1916; joined Staff, as G.S.O. 3, September 3rd, 1917; mentioned in despatches (thrice); M.C. and bar; twice wounded, the second time at Houlthulst Forest on March 8th, 1918, from which he died on June 17th, 1918.

†KIDNER, Corpl. F. E. ... ... 1901-6 *b*

The London Regiment; came home from Russia and joined 16th Bn. (Queen's Westminster Rifles); landed in France, January 26th, 1915; died, February 20th, 1916, of wounds received near Armentières, February 19th.

*KIDNER, Major W. E. ... 1897-1901 *b*

Royal Engineers; 2nd Queen Victoria's Own Sappers and Miners; 33rd Divl. Signal Coy., Lahore Division; I.E.F., January, 1915, to October, 1915; trained 40th Divl. Signal Coy., and took it to France, June 1st, 1916; recalled to India, October, 1917; General Staff; M.C.

†KING, 2nd Lieut. E. W. ... 1893-9 *a*

Royal Field Artillery; came over from F.M.S. to join up, in August, 1917; went to France, April, 1918; wounded, October 19th, 1918, and died next day.

*KINGSTONE, Capt. J. J. ... ... 1906-11 *a*

2nd Dragoon Guards (Queen's Bays); Staff-Capt., 1st Cavalry Brigade; served in France from August 14th, 1914, to 1919; mentioned in despatches (twice); M.C.; D.S.O.

KIRKWOOD, Pte. J. T. ... ... 1893-6 *f*

Royal Air Force; served in France with observation balloons.

KIRTON, Lieut. K. S. ... ... 1910-12 *d*

Royal Army Service Corps; attached to 47th Brigade, Royal Garrison Artillery, in France; formerly in West Somerset Yeomanry, 1st Bn.; served in Gallipoli.

†KITSON, 2nd Lieut. E. G. T. ... 1909-15 *c*
The Duke of Cornwall's Light Infantry; gazetted to 3rd Bn. (Reserve), August 14th, 1915; went to France, March, 1916, and joined 6th Entrenching Bn.; attached 1st Bn., June, 1916; died, September 3rd, 1916, from wounds received the same day, at Guillemont, in the Battle of the Somme.

KNIGHT, Corpl. J. E. ... ... 1903-4 *a*
Royal Field Artillery.

*KNOBEL, Capt. H. E. ... ... 1885-90 *a*
Staff-Capt., 2nd Canadian Infantry Brigade; gassed at Ypres; invalided out, April, 1917; mentioned in despatches (twice).

KNÖS, Capt. J. E. ... ... 1910-13 *d*
2nd Worcestershire (Queen's Own Worcestershire Hussars); wounded at Beersheba, November 8th, 1917.

*KNOX, Major J. H. ... ... 1899-1905 *f*
Honourable Artillery Company, 'A' Battery; attached to Royal Garrison Artillery; wounded; M.C.

KRAUSE, Lieut. E. H. ... ... 1905-11 *d*
The Durham Light Infantry, 10th Bn.

KRAUSE, Pte. R. A. ... ... 1912-16 *d*
The Royal Fusiliers (City of London Regiment), 5th Bn.

*LACEY, Major C. D. ... ... 1897-1900 *a*
The King's Royal Rifle Corps, 9th (S.) Bn.; mentioned in despatches (thrice); M.C.

†LACEY, 2nd Lieut. E. S. ... ... 1901-5 *a*
The Duke of Cambridge's Own (Middlesex Regiment), 16th (S.) Bn. (Public Schools), as Private, in September, 1914; commissioned to 11th Bn., Cheshire Regiment; missing since October 21st, 1916, presumed killed.

LAMB, Major D. G. ... ... 1886-8 *b*
The Rifle Brigade (The Prince Consort's Own); 2nd in Command, 14th (S.) Bn.; served in France, with 1st Bn.; commanded a composite battalion in 4th Division; invalided home in 1917; 2nd in Command, Reserve Bn., The Rifle Brigade.

*LAMBERT, Lieut.-Col. W. J. ... 1887-92 *a*
The King's (Liverpool Regt.); Commanding 14th (S.) Bn. (temp.); 29th Lancers (Deccan Horse), Indian Army; mentioned in despatches; D.S.O. and two bars.

LANE, Gunner D. H. ... ... 1912-16 *f*
Royal Field Artillery, 'A' Battery, 6th Reserve Brigade.

†LARGE, Capt. H. E. ... ... 1894-7 *d*
The Rifle Brigade (The Prince Consort's Own), 10th (S.) Bn.; died, October 9th, 1915, of wounds received that day, near Laventie, France.

†LARNDER, Lieut. E. M. ... ... 1907-12 *f*
West India Regiment; with 1st Bn. at Sierra Leone at out-break of war. After trying all other means of getting to the front, he resigned his Commission in September, 1916, came to England, and enlisted in the 6th Dorsets in October, 1916; went to France in December, 1916; killed in action in front of Arras, April 23rd, 1917 (rank, Private).

*LAURIE, Major H. ... ... 1888-93 *a*

Supt., Remount Squadrons; O.B.E.; mentioned for War Services.

*LAW, Capt. R. W. R. ... ... 1896-7 *b*

The King's Royal Rifle Corps (60th Rifles); Staff-Capt., Headquarters, Southern District, Cork, Ireland; O.B.E.; M.C.

*LECKIE, Lieut.-Col. V. C. ... 1898-1902 *f*

Royal Army Veterinary Corps; Commanding No. 15 Veterinary Hospital, Rouen; mentioned in despatches; D.S.O.

LEE, 2nd Lieut. C. J. ... ... 1914-16 *d*

The Devonshire Regiment, 1st Bn.

LEEDS, 2nd Lieut. H. J. ... 1905-8 *a*

Royal Field Artillery.

†LEEDS, 2nd Lieut J. S. ... ... 1901-5 *a*

Honourable Artillery Company, Infantry; came from Argentine to join the H.A.C., September, 1914; given Commission in H.A.C., December, 1914; went to France, July, 1915; killed in the Crater at Hooge, September 19th, 1915.

*LEEDS, Bt. Lieut-Col. T. L. ... 1883-6 *a*

Indian Army, 59th Scinde Rifles (Frontier Force); served in Mesopotamia; mentioned in despatches (thrice); C.M.G.; D.S.O.

*LEE-WARNER, Rev. A. ... ... 1893-7 *a*

Chaplain to Forces (T.), 1916; Senior C.F. (T.), 1918; Attached Cheshire Regiment, 1st Bn.; mentioned in despatches.

*LEE-WARNER, Lieut.-Col. H. G. 1896-1900 *a*

Royal Field Artillery, 41st Brigade; mentioned in despatches (twice); D.S.O.; M.C.

LEE-WARNER, 2nd Lieut. J. ... 1903-8 *a*

The Northumberland Fusiliers, 2nd Garrison Bn.

*LEGGE, F. C. ... ... ... 1886-92 *a*

Indian Defence Force; East Indian Railway, 1/37th Bn.; Deputy Coal Controller, Calcutta; C.B.E.

†LEGGE, Capt. R. G. ... ... 1892-6 *a*

The Devonshire Regiment, 2nd Bn.; killed in France, December 18th, 1914.

*LE HUQUET, Capt. and Bt. Major R. 1901-5 *d*

The Bedfordshire Regiment, 3rd Bn.; in Command of 8th Bn. from June, 1917, to February, 1918, when disbanded; wounded, May 13th, 1918, when in command 6th Bn., Northamptonshire Regiment; mentioned in despatches.

†LEIGH, 2nd Lieut. H. G. T. ... 1899-1902 *a*

Labour Corps, France; previously served in German S.W. Africa with 8th African Artillery; also in Artillery Cadet School, Leckfield; died in France, November 11th, 1919, from pneumonia.

*LEIGH, Capt. (a./Major) H. V., M.B., B.S., M.R.C.S., L.R.C.P. ... ... 1900-4 *a*

R.A.M.C.; Registrar, successively, of Nos. 31, 27 and 71, General Hospitals; from August, 1917, Officer in Charge, Medical Division, No. 71, General Hospital; mentioned in despatches.

LEONARD, 2nd Lieut. R. F. W. ... 1914-18 *a*
Royal Field Artillery.

LESLIE, Col. P. N. ... ... 1882-5 *Price*
Indian Army.

LETHBRIDGE, 2nd Lieut. A. B. ... 1893-4 *a*
Interpreter.

LETHBRIDGE, Lieut. J. C. B. ... 1901-11 *b*
Royal 1st Devon Yeomanry (T.F.); served in Egypt and France from January 1st, 1916, to March, 1919.

*LEWIS, Capt. (Bt. Major, acting Lt.-Col.) F. E. C. ... ... ... 1908-12 *a*
The East Lancashire Regiment; attached 47th Machine Gun Battalion; mentioned in despatches (twice).

LEWIS, Pte. H. E. C. ... ... 1912-13 *c*
The Prince of Wales's (North Staffordshire Regiment), 6th Bn.

*LEY, Capt. C. E. A. ... ... 1902-6 *c*
Joined the Canadian Contingent, 1914; joined R.E. at home, 1915, and went with Egyptian Expeditionary Force to Palestine same year; gained M.C. at taking of Jerusalem; placed in charge of Telegraphs in Aleppo district.

*LEY, Lieut.-Col. E. M. ... 1898-1902 *a*
The King's Royal Rifle Corps, 3rd Bn.; mentioned in despatches; D.S.O.

LEY, Capt. R. H. ... ... 1895-8 *a*
Canadian Expeditionary Force; 88th Victoria Fusiliers; joined Balloon Section in Palestine Campaign.

LEYBORNE-POPHAM, Capt. and Adjt. F. H. A. ... ... ... 1905-8 *d*

The Bedfordshire Regiment, 6th (S.) Bn.

†*LIMBERY, Capt. C. R. ... ... 1905-8 *d*

The South Staffordshire Regiment, 1st Bn.; went to France with 1st B.E.F., August, 1914, and was twice wounded at Loos, and again in May, 1916; mentioned in despatches; M.C.; killed at Mametz, July 1st, 1916.

†*LIMBERY, Capt. K. T. ... ... 1905-10 *d*

R.A.M.C.; went to France as a dresser, September 4th, 1914; to Russia with an Ambulance, October, 1915; to France again, March, 1916; mentioned in despatches; M.C.; killed in action, September 26th, 1917.

*LINDLEY, Lieut. (a./Capt.) W. M. 1905-7 *d*

Royal Engineers (T.F.); Officer Commanding 8th Corps Heavy Artillery, Signals; served in France continuously from November 6th, 1914; mentioned in despatches; M.C.

LLEWELLIN, Lieut. E. C. ... 1908-12 *d*

The Monmouthshire Regiment, 1/1st Bn.; wounded at St. Julian, April 25th, 1915.

†LLEWELLIN, 2nd Lieut. W. M. J. 1913-16 *a*

The South Wales Borderers, 1st Bn.; went from School to Sandhurst, January, 1917; gazetted 2nd Lieut., December, 1917; went to France, April, 1918; wounded, June, 1918; killed, on patrol at Cambrai, August 17th, 1918.

†LLOYD, 2nd Lieut. G. L. B. ... 1912-14 *Master*
The Dorsetshire Regiment, 5th (S.) Bn.; killed, August 6th, 1915, in the landing at Suvla Bay, Gallipoli.

LOCKWOOD, 2nd Lieut. D. D. ... 1912-16 *b*
Royal Air Force.

LONSDALE, Capt. P. ... ... 1886-90 *d*
East Lancashire Regiment (Reserve of Officers); 1st Class District Officer, N. Provinces, Nigeria.

LOTT, 2nd Lieut. D. B. ... ... 1914-18 *f*
12th Officer Cadet Bn.; attached 3rd Bn., The Bedfordshire Regiment.

†*LOTT, Lieut. J. C. ... ... 1908-13 *f*
The Royal Fusiliers (City of London Regiment), 18th (S.) 1st Public Schools' Bn. (Special Reserve of Officers), and The East Lancashire Regt., 3rd Bn., attached 11th Bn.; wounded, March, 1917, and March, 1918; killed in action in France, April 13th, 1918; M.C.

*LOTT, Lieut. R. C. ... ... 1906-11 *f*
The Lancashire Fusiliers, 12th (S.) Bn.; wounded (in Macedonia), September, 1916; mentioned in despatches; attached General Staff, War Office, August, 1917; mentioned for War Services.

*LOVEBAND, Col. F. R. ... ... 1877-82 *a*
West India Regiment (Bt.-Col.) (Reserve of Officers); The Prince of Wales's Own (West Yorkshire Regiment); Commanding 1st Garrison Bn.; mentioned for War Services.

Low, Rev. P. W. ... ... 1896-1901 *b*

52nd Brigade (Infantry), 17th Division (Army Chaplains' Department).

Lowis, Lieut.-Col. F. C., C.I.E. ... 1886-91 *d*

Royal Engineers; served in Persia.

†*Luard, Lieut.-Col. E. B. ... 1884 *c*

The King's Shropshire Light Infantry, 1st Bn.; mentioned in despatches (thrice); D.S.O.; mortally wounded, April 21st, 1916, at the re-taking of the Ypres Langemark Trenches; died, April 24th, 1916.

Luard, Lieut.-Col. G. D. ... 1880-3 *c*

The Cameronians (Scottish Rifles).

Lucas, Lieut. D. ... ... 1901-6 *a*

Honourable Artillery Company; mentioned for War Services.

Luff, Lieut. C. M. C. ... ... 1912-14 *a*

Royal Army Service Corps.

*Lumley, Capt. D. O. ... ... 1909-13 *d*

The Duke of Edinburgh's (Wiltshire Regiment), 5th (S.) Bn.; served in Gallipoli; wounded, July 23rd, 1915; Deputy Assistant Inspector of Recruiting, Southern Command, April 25th, 1916, to September 13th, 1917; then employed at War Office; transferred to General List for duty with Ministry of National Service; Head of Registration Branch, August 1st, 1918; O.B.E.

Lund, Capt. R. J. S. ... ... 1910-13 *a*

Princess Charlotte of Wales's (Royal Berkshire Regiment), 1/4th Bn. (T.); 60th Squadron, Royal Air Force.

*LUNT, Rev. G. C. L. ... 1899-1905 *a*

Temporary Chaplain to the Forces, B.E.F. (1917); M.C.

*LUSH, Rev. J. A. ... ... 1898-1900 *c*

Chaplain to the Forces; served in France; attached to 2nd Canterbury Regiment, N.Z.E.F.; mentioned in despatches.

*LUTTMAN-JOHNSON, Capt. H. M. ... 1888-92 *a*

Lieut., Royal West Kent Regiment, December, 1914, to May, 1915; Lieut., R.E., May, 1915; Capt., R.E., July, 1916; wounded, October, 1916; mentioned in despatches.

*MACARTNEY-FILGATE, Lieut.-Col. A. R. P. H. ... ... 1886-9 *Price*

The Royal Welsh Fusiliers, 3rd Bn. (Res.); O.B.E. (Military).

MACCARTHY, Midshipman G. ... 1910-15 *Prep.*

Royal Navy; 1917, H.M.S. Collingwood.

MACCOLL, Flight Sub-Lieut. A.J.H. 1909-11 *f*

Royal Navy.

*MACDONALD, Lieut.-Col. I. T. A. 1897-1901 *T*

Royal Army Service Corps; Assistant Director, Department of Local Resources, Mesopotamia Expeditionary Force; mentioned in despatches (twice); O.B.E.

*MACGILLYCUDDY, Capt. A. R. N. ... 1901-5 *b*

R.A.M.C., French Base Hospital; M.C.

MACKINTOSH, Lieut. H. S. ... 1912-14 *a*

R.H.A.; 'K' Battery, No. 8 Res. Brigade; served in France with 'B' Battery, 83rd Brigade, R.F.A., 18th Division.

†*MACWHIRTER, Major T. ... 1900-2 *b*
The Gordon Highlanders, 9th (S.) Bn. (Pioneers); wounded twice; M.C.; killed on the Arras Front, April 27th, 1917.

*MAIR, Capt. (Bt. Major and temp. Lieut.-Col.) J. A. F. ... ... ... 1902-5 *d*
East Yorkshire Regiment; Army Signal Service; Chief Signal Officer, 11th Corps; mentioned in despatches; M.C.

MAIR, Capt. R. P. ... ... 1899-1904 *d*
Sussex Yeomanry, 1st Bn.; attached to 11th Royal Sussex Regiment; served with North Russia Expeditionary Force.

MAIS, Lieut. S. P. B. ... ... 1913-17 *Master*
Unattached List (T.F.), Sherborne O.T.C., 1913 to 1917; Tonbridge O.T.C., 1917.

*MALONE, Lieut.-Col. C. R. R. ... 1874-6 *a*
Ret. Pay; since September, 1914, was successively Adjutant, 7th Bn., and 2nd in Command of 13th Bn., and in Command of 14th Bn., Worcestershire Regiment, and 15th (S.) Bn. and 16th (Reserve T.) Bn., The Hampshire Regiment; reverted to retired pay, with rank of Lieut.-Col., Nov. 17th, 1917; mentioned for war services.

MANN, R. H. ... ... ... 1912-17 *d*
Bristol University O.T.C. and No. 1, R.G.A. Officers' Cadet School, Tonbridge.

†MANSEL-PLEYDELL, Lieut. E. M. ... 1903-5 *f*
The Dorsetshire Regiment; joined 3rd Bn., August, 1914; went to France, Jan., 1915, attached Worcestershire Regiment; killed at Kemmel, Flanders, March 12th, 1915.

†MARSH, Capt. and Adjt. E. W. H. 1893-7 *a*

Indian Army; 13th Rajputs (The Skekhawati Regiment); drowned on the Persia, December 30th, 1915.

†MARSON, 2nd Lieut. J. C. ... 1910-13 *d*

1st September, 1914, gazetted to 6th Bn., Loyal N. Lancs; was transferred to The Welsh Regiment, 8th (S.) Bn. (Pioneers); went to the Dardanelles, June 15th, 1915; killed at Suvla Bay, August 8th, 1915.

†MARTIN, 2nd Lieut. C. ... ... 1894-6 *d*

Coldstream Guards; killed in action on St. Quentin Ridge, December 1st, 1917.

MARTYN, Lieut. W. W. ... ... 1906-7 *a*

Indian Army; served with 2nd Rajputs, 18th Pioneers, and 116th Mahrattas, in Egypt and Mesopotamia.

*MARWOOD-ELTON, Lieut.-Col. W. 1879-85 *b*

The Welsh Regiment; Commanded 3rd Bn. (Reserve); Garrison Commander of The Severn Garrison, also Competent Military Authority; attached to Labour Corps, March, 1917; served in France and Belgium; mentioned in despatches.

MASON, Capt. B. G. ... ... 1912-15 *a*

Royal Field Artillery; 407th Battery, 96th (Army) Brigade; served in France.

*MASON, Lieut. (a./Capt.) I. N. ... 1907-11 *f*

The Worcestershire Regiment; attached 18th Bn.; M.C.

MASON, Corpl. J. C. ... ... 1891-4 *c*

Army Pay Corps.

Mason, Capt. W. M. ... ... 1910-14 *f*
The South Wales Borderers, 2nd Bn.

*Mathew, Lieut. C. G. ... ... 1908-9 *c*
The Devonshire Regt., 10th Bn.; served in Salonika; mentioned in despatches.

Matterson, Capt. S. K. ... 1890-93 *d*
Army Remount Service; 47th Remount Squadron; served in France and Egypt.

Matterson, Lieut. W. A. K. ... 1888-93 *d*
Territorial Force Reserve.

*Maunsell, Capt. F. H. R. ... 1901-6 *a*
The King's Shropshire Light Infantry; wounded, November, 1914, and (slightly), October, 1915; mentioned in despatches.

†Maunsell, Capt. R. G. F. ... 1904-8 *a*
Royal Engineers (T.F.), 1/7th Field Company, Hants; drowned, May 4th, 1917, on the way to Salonika, when the transport, 'Transylvania,' was torpedoed in the Mediterranean.

*May, Surgeon Vice-Admiral Sir A. W., K.C.B., K.H.P., F.R.C.S. ... 1868-71 *b*
Late Director-General of the Medical Department of the Navy; Commander of Order of Leopold; Order of the Sacred Treasure (Japan), 1st Class.

May, Capt. C. M. N. ... ... 1888-9 *c*
S.A.M.C., South African Contingent.

May, Major G. W. G. ... 1896-1900 *d*
The Cheshire Regiment, 3rd Bn. (Res.); attached Headquarters, Western Command, Chester.

†MAY, Lieut. H. G. ... { 1902-7 *d* / 1914 *Master*

The Dorsetshire Regiment, 3rd Bn. (Res.), attached 1st Bn.; died, March 28th, 1915, of wounds received at St. Eloi, March 14th.

†MAY, Lieut. T. R. A. ... ... 1913-17 *a*

Royal Air Force; killed in France, August 9th, 1918.

MAYBURY, Cadet M. ... ... 1914-18 *d*

Cambridge University O.T.C.

MAYES, Rev. R. M. ... ... 1898-1900 *b*

S.C.F., Guards' Repôt, Caterham.

MAYO, Capt. C. W. ... ... 1893-8 *a*

The Royal Sussex Regiment, 13th (S.) Bn. (3rd South Down).

MAYO, 2nd Lieut. J. T. ... ... 1913-17 *c*

The Dorsetshire Regiment.

McCLELLAN, 2nd Lieut. J. F. M. ... 1910-12 *f*

Tank Corps.

McCLELLAN, Capt. N. G. C. ... 1903-8 *a*

The Royal Welsh Fusiliers, 3rd Bn. (Reserve), attached Welsh Regiment.

McCREA, 2nd Lieut. F. W. W. ... 1912-14 *g*

The Devonshire Regiment, 2nd Bn.; wounded, January 6th, 1918.

*McCULLAGH, Capt. A. C. H., M.D., B.S. ... ... ... 1897-1900 *a*

T.F. (Reserve); D.S.O.

*McCullagh, Capt. (a./Lieut.-Col.) H. R. ... ... ... 1894-9 *a*

The Durham Light Infantry, 1st Bn.; served in India till December, 1916; then with 2nd Bn., in France; 2nd in Command 8th Bn., The Bedfordshire Regiment, April to August, 1917; then a./Lieut.-Col. in Command 2nd Bn., D.L.I.; transferred to 19th Bn., D.L.I., 1918; mentioned in despatches (thrice); D.S.O.

McEnery, E. H. ... ... 1890-4 *T.*

British Red Cross; in France.

†McEnery, Capt. J. A. ... ... 1890-4 *T. & b*

Royal Engineers; O.C. of 54th Co.; landed in Belgium with Sir Henry Rawlinson's Division for the relief of Antwerp, and was killed at Yser, October 26th, 1914.

*McEnery, Major (a./Lieut.-Col.) R.T. ... ... ... 1893-8 *T.*

Seistan Field Force; Bt. Lieut.-Col.; mentioned for war services, India.

†McGowan, 2nd Lieut. J. S. ... 1911-15 *f*

The Devonshire Regiment; June, 1915, Commissioned to 3rd Bn.; May 20th, 1916, went to France, attached to 2nd Bn.; killed at La Boiselle on the Somme, July 1st, 1916.

Mein, Bt. Col. J. E. ... ... 1865-7 *a*

Ret. Indian Army; Staff Lieut., G.S.O., 3rd Grade.

Mercer, Capt. L. E. ... ... 1896-9 *f*

The Dorsetshire Regiment, 3rd Bn. (Res.); served in France, May, 1917, to October, 1918; retired, December 18th, 1918.

MERRIMAN, 2nd Lieut. F. V. ... 1900-6 *a*

Royal Army Medical Corps; War Hospital, Norwich; Censors Staff at Dunkirk.

MERRIMAN, Pte. T. F. ... ... 1904-9 *a*

Royal Army Medical Corps.

MILLER, Sapper A. O. ... ... 1909-12 *T.*

1st Canadian Railway Troops; wounded at Hooge, April 4th, 1916, when serving (as Trooper) with 1st Canadian Mounted Rifles.

MILLER, 2nd Lieut. H. ... ... 1911-13 *T.*

Tank Corps, 'C' Company, 4th Bn.; served as Trooper in 1st Dorset (Queen's Own) Yeomanry, in Egypt and Gallipoli, till wounded on September 2nd, 1915; on recovery did home service with 2nd Dorset Yeomanry; gazetted to Tank Corps, January 31st, 1918; served in France from May 29th, 1918.

†MILLIGAN, 2nd Lieut. A. ... 1912-15 *f*

Princess Louise's (Argyll and Sutherland Highlanders); September, 1915, Commissioned to 3rd Bn. (Reserve); kept at Dreghorn as Bombing Officer till he was 19, and went to France in January, 1917, attached to 7th Bn.; died on May 30th, 1917, from wounds received on May 27th, 1917, during the second advance in the first battle of Arras.

MILLIGAN, 2nd Lieut. W. R. ... 1912-17 *b*

The Highland Light Infantry, 1st (Res.) Gr. Bn.

*MOBERLEY, Major and Bt. Lieut.-Col. A. H. ... ... ... 1893-6 *a*

Royal Garrison Artillery; mentioned in despatches (thrice); D.S.O.; Military Order of Savoy (Chevalier); Order of St. Maurice & St. Lazarus; Légion d'Honneur.

MOBERLY, Corpl. R. E. ... ... 1911-15 *g*

Royal Devon Yeomanry, 1st Bn. (T.F).

MOCKETT, Major H. B. ... ... 1895-7 *d*

4th (Queen's Own)) Hussars; served in France; wounded, September 13th, 1914; incapacitated by illness contracted on Active Service, from December, 1917, to October, 1918.

MOCKRIDGE, Lieut. A. H. ... 1912-16 *d*

Royal Field Artillery; served in France with 303rd Siege Battery; aad at Bonn (Germany) with Army of Occupation.

MOLONY, Lieut. J. T. ... ... 1908-10 *f*

The Dorsetshire Regiment, 1/4th Bn.(T.); attached The Oxfordshire and Buckinghampshire Light Infantry; served in India and Mesopotamia.

MONCKTON, Lieut. J. P.... ... 1906-9 *a*

South Nottinghamshire Hussars.

MONKHOUSE, 2nd Lieut. G. A. ... 1899-1901 *f*

The Buffs (East Kent Regiment), 1st (F.S.) Gr. Bn.

*MONRO, Gen. Sir C. C., K.C.B. ... 1871-3 *a*

The Queen's (Royal West Surrey) Regiment; Commanding 1st Army, B.E.F.; Commander-in-Chief in India; A.D.C. General to the King; mentioned in despatches (thrice); Légion d'Honneur (Grand Officer); G.C.B., G.C.M.G., G.C.S.I.; Knight of Grace of Order of Hospital of St. John of Jerusalem.

†MONTGOMERIE, Capt. W. G. ... 1893-4 *a*

The Prince of Wales's Leinster Regiment (Royal Canadians); died, October 20th, 1914, of wounds received near Armentières, October 18th.

MOORE, Major C. G. H. ... 1899-1903 *c*

R.A.M.C.; mentioned for War Services.

*MOORE, Lieut.-Comdr. H. R. ... 1895-99 *Prep.*

Royal Navy; D.S.O.

†MOORE, 2nd Lieut. R. ... ... 1907-13 *a*

The Rifle Brigade (The Prince Consort's Own), 10th Bn.; after several rejections was accepted by Public School Corps; made Sergt., and went to France at end of 1915; transferred to Cadet Corps at Oxford in Spring of 1916; gazetted to Royal Sussex in July, 1916; transferred to Middlesex Regiment, went again to France, October, 1916, and was transferred to Rifle Brigade; died in France on August 15th, 1917, from wounds received in action the previous day, at the forcing of the Steenbeek, in front of Langemark.

†MOORE, Trooper R. T. ... ... 1907-8 *b*

Royal Wiltshire Yeomanry (Prince of Wales's Own Royal Regiment); drowned in the Leinster on his way home on leave, October, 1918.

*MOORE, Capt. T. ... ... 1897-1900 *a*

Prince Albert's (Somerset Light Infantry), 1/5th Bn. (T.); served in Mesopotamia; mentioned in despatches.

MORE, Lieut. R. McL. ... ... 1913-15 *d*

Royal Garrison Artillery; served with 5th Siege Battery in France.

MORGAN, Lieut. P. R. J. ... 1912-13 *f*

Royal Engineers (T.F.); No. 1, Works Company, Kent Fortress Engineers.

†MORITZ, 2nd Lieut. O. F. ... 1898-1903 *c*

Enlisted in R.A.M.C., September 4th, 1914; 1915, Commissioned to The Border Regiment, 10th Bn.; transferred to Machine Gun Corps (99th) in same year; went to France, April, 1916; killed at Delville Wood, July 27th, 1916, while trying to bring up reinforcements for his gun.

*MORRISON, Capt. M. J. ... ... 1907-12 *a*

The Durham Light Infantry, 1/5th Bn. (T.); M.C., with two bars.

*MORTON, Lieut. C. W. ... ... 1910-14 *b*

The Worcestershire Regt., 4th Bn.; M.C.

MORTON, Lieut. R. J. ... ... 1909-14 *b*

The Duke of Cambridge's Own (Middlesex Regiment), 2/9th Bn. (T), attached 2/10th Bn. (T.); 14th Squadron Royal Air Force.

Moser, Capt. H. B. ... ... 1897-1900 *a*
The Cheshire Regiment, 9th (S.) Bn.

Moulton-Barrett, 2nd Lieut. E.S. 1909-12 *d*
Seaforth Highlanders (Ross-shire Buffs, The Duke of Albany's); Royal Flying Corps.

Mulock, Cadet J. S. ... ... 1914-17 *f*
Royal Air Force.

*Murray, Major E. M. ... ... 1893-8 *f*
Special Reserve, 16th Lancers; served in Gallipoli, 1915, as Adjutant of 1/2nd Scottish Horse; in Egypt, 1916; in France, 1917-18; mentioned in despatches.

†Murray, Major T. F. ... ... 1887-91 *a*
The Highland Light Infantry, 1st Bn. (Indian Expeditionary Force); killed at the battle of Festubert, December 20th, 1914.

*Muspratt, Capt. C. K. ... ... 1906-12 *a*
The Hampshire Regiment, 2/7th Bn. (T.); served in India, December, 1914; in Mesopotamia since September, 1917; mentioned in despatches.

†*Muspratt, Capt. K. K. ... 1911-16 *a*
The Dorsetshire Regiment, attached to R.F.C.; served in France, 1917; M.C.; killed flying on duty in Suffolk, March 16th, 1918.

†*Muspratt, Capt. T. P. ... 1910-13 *a*
Gazetted to The Worcestershire Regiment, 3rd Bn., in August, 1914; went to France, September 8th, 1914; wounded in the first battle of the Aisne on September 20th, 1914; was temporary Capt. from June,

1915, at the battle of Hooge, onwards; wounded again, April, 1916, on Vimy Ridge; mentioned in despatches; M.C.; died on May 29th, 1918, of wounds received the same day, near Rheims.

MYRES, 2nd Lieut. M. C. ... 1913-18 *a*

No. 2, Cavalry Cadet School, and No. 4, Cavalry Reserve (Dragoons).

*NAPIER, 2nd Lieut. W. ... ... 1903-5 *d*

Royal Army Service Corps; mentioned in despatches.

*NEWMARCH, Col. B. J., V.D. ... 1871-3 *b*

Australian Army Medical Corps; in command 1st Australian Field Ambulance, 1914; Senior Surgeon, 2nd Australian General Hospital, 1915; in command 1st Australian General Hospital, 1915; in command 3rd Australian General Hospital, 1916; mentioned in despatches; C.M.G., C.B.E. (Military).

NICHOLLS, Major F. L. ... 1897-1901 *a*

The Welsh Regt., 2/7th (Cyclist) Bn. (T.)

NICHOLS, 2nd Lieut. A. A. P. ... 1908-11 *d*

The Gordon Highlanders, 3rd Bn.

NICHOLS, 2nd Lieut. W. N. ... 1907-10 *g*

Cheshire Regiment.

NICOLLS, 2nd Lieut. R. M. ... 1911-12 *g*

Royal Field Artillery, 53rd Brigade.

*NORTH, Capt. E. S. ... ... 1907-11 *a*

The Royal Fusiliers (City of London Regiment), 3rd Bn.; mentioned in despatches.

*Northcroft, Lieut. E. G. D. ... 1910-15 *c*

The Bedfordshire Regiment, 5th Bn., and 84th Machine Gun Coy.; seconded to Machine Gun Corps, May, 1918; served in France and Salonika; twice wounded; mentioned in despatches.

†*Northey, Lieut. A. ... ... 1900-4 *f*

The Worcestershire Regiment, 4th Bn.; mentioned in despatches; killed at Richebourg St. Vaast, October 12th, 1914.

*Notley, Lieut.-Col. W. K. ... 1893-8 *T.*

Commissioner East Africa Police; temp. Lieut.-Col. Provost Marshal and Officer Administering Martial Law, B.E.A., from August 6th, 1914, to January 22nd, 1919; mentioned in despatches; D.S.O.; Cavalier Order of St. Maurice and St. Lazarus (Italy).

†Nutter, 2nd Lieut. G. H. E. ... 1913-17 *a*

Machine Gun Corps, December, 1917, commissioned; March, 1918, went to France to M.G.C. of 19th Div.; killed at Beaumetz, France, March 23rd, 1918.

*Nutting, Capt. A. F. ... ... 1904-8 *f*

The King's Royal Rifle Corps, 11 (S.) Bn.; M.C. and bar.

Nutting, Capt. L. B. ... ... 1900-2 *a*

Remount Service; Asst. Superintendent Remount Squadrons; served in France, 1915-17.

*O'Hanlon, Capt. G. ... ... 1908-*Master*

The Dorsetshire Regiment, 6th (S.) Bn.; served in France, July, 1915, to October, 1918; 18th and 8th Corps Schools Instructor, April, 1917, to October, 1918; M.C.

OLDNALL, 2nd Lieut. H. R. ... 1913-16 *g*
The Worcester Regiment, 1st & 5th Bns.; served in France; gassed at Vimy Ridge.

*OLLIVANT, Major G. B. ... ... 1893-4 *a*
12th (Prince of Wales's Royal) Lancers (Special Reserve); Bt. Major; mentioned in despatches.

OLIVER, Major J. F. ... ... 1890-2 *d*
The Manchester Regiment, 11th (S.) Bn.

OLIVER, Lieut.-Comdr. T. L. ... 1883-7 *c*
Enlisted in Sportsman's Bn.; invalided out; joined R.N.V.R., attached R.N.A.S.

†OLLIVIER, Major G. L. ... ... 1900-2 *d*
Royal Garrison Artillery, 6th Siege Battery; went to France, September, 1914; wounded three times; died of wounds in Hospital, France, January 20th, 1918.

O'MEARA, Lieut.-Col. E. J., F.R.C.S. 1889-92 *T.*
Indian Medical Service.

†OPENSHAW, Capt. G. O. ... ... 1904-8 *f*
Royal Army Service Corps; attached 2nd Division; wounded and taken prisoner, May 27th, 1918; died of wounds, August 9th, 1918, at Rastatt, Germany.

ORMSBY, Major T. ... ... 1884 *Price*
Army Pay Department; Staff-Paymaster.

*OSTLE, Capt. D. W. ... ... 1907-10 *a*
Royal Army Service Corps; mentioned in despatches.

*PADWICK, Surgeon H. B. ... 1904-8 *d*
Royal Navy; D.S.O.

PAGDEN, Sub-Lieut. F. L. K. ... 1908-10 *Prep.*
Royal Navy.

PAGE, Capt. D. C. ... ... 1910-12 *c*
Royal Air Force.

PAGE, 2nd Lieut. K. E. ... ... 1910-13 *a*
The Duke of Cambridge's Own (Middlesex Regiment), 5th Bn. (Special Reserve); wounded in the head at Monchy-le-Preux, April 27th, 1917; invalided out, May 23rd, 1918.

†PALMER, Sub-Lieut. E. J. ... 1905-8 *a*
Volunteered, August, 1914, rejected (defective eyesight); joined Friends' Ambulance in France; gazetted September, 1915, to Royal Naval Division, 'Nelson' Bn.; died on April 27th, 1917, of wounds received on April 23rd, 1917; buried at Aubigny, France.

PALMER, H. R. C. ... ... 1903-6 *a*
Royal Naval Experimental Service; Mechanic.

†PALMER, Lieut. L. S. ... ... 1906-9 *a*
The Dorsetshire Regiment, 3/4th Bn. (T); attached to 117th Machine Gun Company; killed, September 20th, 1917, at Shrewsbury Forest, France.

PALMER, Lieut. N. L. L. ... 1912-15 *a*
Royal Horse Artillery, 'Y' Battery; served in France with 1st Cavalry Division.

*PARHAM, Capt. H. J. ... ... 1909-13 *a*

Royal Field Artillery; mentioned in despatches (twice); Croix de Guerre (French).

PARISH, Capt. A. B. O. ... ... 1906-9 *d*

The Lincolnshire Regiment, 3rd Bn.

PARK, Lieut. R. H. M. ... ... 1892-7 *d*

Irish Guards.

†*PARRY, Lieut.-Col. C. F. P. ... 1884-6 *d*

Royal Field Artillery, 136th Battery; O.C. 34th Brigade, R.F.A.; served in France from November 5th, 1914, to August 20th, 1918; wounded, August 3rd, 1917; mentioned in despatches (four times); D.S.O.; killed, August 20th, 1918.

PARRY, Capt. G. P. ... ... 1884-6 *d*

Called out during rebellion in South Africa, but found unfit for service, owing to ill-health, the result of service during Boer War.

†*PARRY-JONES, Capt. O. G., M.R.C.S., L.R.C.P. ... ... ... 1900-6 *f*

R.A.M.C. (late 2nd Lieut., Reserve of Officers); Special Reserve; attached Lancashire Fusiliers; Lieut., R.A M.C., January, 1915; Capt., May, 1915; France, July, 1915; attached Suffolk Regiment; mentioned in despatches; died of wounds received at Stuff Redoubt, Thiepval, Oct. 29th, 1916.

PARRY-JONES, 2nd Lieut. M. B. ... 1912-17 *f*

Royal Garrison Artillery; served in France with 81st Siege Battery.

PARRY-JONES, Capt. P. E. H. ... 1906-11 *f*

South Wales Borderers, 5th Bn.; France, July, 1915; wounded, July 26th, 1916, at Mametz Wood; Musketry Instructor, 3rd Bn., S.W.B., April to October, 1917; Instructor, 19th O.C.B., Pirbright, November, 1917, to November, 1918.

PARSONS, Lieut. C. P. ... ... 1911-15 *d*

Royal Air Force; previously in R.A.M.C. and The Wiltshire Regiment; served in India, Mesopotamia and Egypt.

PARSONS, Capt. G. L. ... ... 1887-9 *c*

R.A.M.C.; September, 1915, M.O., Military Hospital, Millbank; December, 1915, M.O., 30th General Hospital, Medical Expeditionary Force; March, 1916, M.O., 16th General Hospital, France; July, 1916, M.O., 1st Worcesters, France; October, 1917, M.O., 11th and 19th, Officers' Cadet Bns., Aldershot; April, 1918, O.C., 5th Ambulance Train, France.

†PARSONS, Capt. M. H. D. ... 1895-8 *a*

Royal Horse Artillery, 'O' Battery, 8th Division; killed in action, in France, July 19th, 1916.

*PARTRIDGE, Lieut.-Col. L. ... 1892-7 *c*

Pembroke (Castlemartin) Yeomanry (T.F.); late 3rd Dragoon Guards; mentioned in despatches; D.S.O.; Order of the Nile; Légion d'Honneur (Chevalier).

*PARTRIDGE, Major N. H. E. ... 1887-90 *b*

Royal Army Service Corps; served in France and Italy; mentioned in despatches (twice).

PASLEY, 2nd Lieut. R. M. S. ... 1913-17 *d*

Royal Field Artillery.

PATERSON, Lieut. F. S. ... ... 1883-7 *b*

Royal Engineers (T.F.); o/c. Signals, Forth Fortress Coy. R.E., December, 1918.

PATERSON, 2nd Lieut. H. R. ... 1912-17 *b*

Royal Field Artillery, 4th 'B' Reserve Brigade.

PEDDIE, Major G. ... ... 1886-9 *c*

Hyderabad Volunteers.

*PEELE, Lieut. C. R. de C. ... 1908-10 *b*

55th Coke's Rifles (Frontier Force); served in Mesopotamia; mentioned in despatches.

*PELLY, Capt. F. Brian ... ... 1903-8 *a*

Royal Navy; attached to 6th Wing R.N.A.S.; to 66th Wing R.A.F., April 1st, 1918; to 67th Wing, June 23rd, 1918, for Intelligence Officer's duties; to Army Council, for Secretarial duties, January 1st, 1919; A.F.C.

*PENDAVIS, Lieut. H. V. ... ... 1909-10 *b*

The Oxfordshire and Buckinghamshire Light Infantry, 5/2nd Bn.; attached Royal Flying Corps (1915), France and Flanders; Egypt (1918), as Instructor in War Flying; mentioned in despatches; D.S.O.

PENMAN, 2nd Lieut. G. G. ... 1914-17 *d*

Royal Field Artillery.

*PENNEFATHER, Capt. and Adjt. J. B. 1904-9 *c*

The Loyal North Lancashire Regiment, 6th (S.) Bn.; served in Gallipoli and with Mesopotamia Expeditionary Force (M.F.O.), 1916 to 1919; wounded, 1916; mentioned in despatches (twice); O.B.E.

†*PENRUDDOCKE, Lieut. C. ... 1907-10 *b*
The Duke of Edinburgh's (Wiltshire Regiment), 7th (S.) Bn.; rejoined Colours at outbreak of war; wounded at Salonika, November, 1917; mentioned in despatches; M.C.; killed in France, October 4th, 1918.

PERROTT, 2nd Lieut. T. H. H. ... 1913-17 *a*
The Worcestershire Regiment.

PETERS, Cadet E. L. du T. ... 1912-15 *f*
Royal Air Force.

PETERS, Pte. J. S. du T. ... 1914-17 *f*
Young Soldiers' Bn., 52nd (Hants Regt.).

PETHERICK, Lieut. H. L. ... 1895-7 *d*
Royal Garrison Artillery.

PHILLIPS, Capt. and Adjt. H. S. ... 1900-3 *a*
Indian Army; 27th Light Cavalry.

*PICK, Surgeon Lieut.-Comdr. B. ... 1893-7 *a*
Royal Navy; R.N. Hospital Haslar; mentioned in despatches.

PIGEON, Lieut. J. W. ... ... 1902-5 *f*
R.A.M.C.; No. 12, Indian General Hospital, I.E.F., 'D'; Indian Medical Service.

PIM, Flight Cadet I. M. ... 1913-18 *a*
Royal Air Force.

PINHEY, Lieut. J. W. ... ... 1905-8 *Prep.*
Royal Navy; 1914, H.M.S. Australian; 1915, H.M.S. Nottingham, in which ship present at battle of Jutland, 1916, Submarined.

PINHEY, Capt. R. A. ... ... 1906-10 *T.*

The Buffs (East Kent Regiment), 3rd Bn., attached 1st Bn.

*PLANT, Major H. F. ... ... 1902-6 *a*

Royal Field Artillery; H.Q., R.A., 55th (West Lancs.) Division; mentioned in despatches; M.C.

PLANT, Lieut. L. H. ... ... 1903-8 *a*

Royal Field Artillery; August 12th, 1914, gazetted to 11th Battery, 2nd West Lancs. Brigade; May, 1915, went to Egypt with 42nd Div. Ammunition Column; March 4th, 1917, attached Royal Flying Corps; July, 1917, R.F.C. Instructor.

PLAYFORD, Lieut. F. D. ... ... 1902-4 *a*

Surrey (Queen Mary's Regiment) Yeomanry (T.F.).

*POOLE, Capt. E. J. E. ... ... 1900-2 *d*

Indian Army; 46th Punjabis; M.C.

†*POORE, Lieut.-Col. R. A., D.S.O. 1885-9 *f*

Royal Wilts Yeomanry (Prince of Wales's Own Royal Regiment) (T.F.); appointed to Command of 2/1st Bn., Royal Wilts Yeomanry, January, 1915; appointed 2nd in Command 2nd Bn. R. Welsh Fusiliers, and later in Command; mentioned in despatches; killed in France, Sept. 26th, 1917.

*POPE, Lieut.-Col. W. W. ... 1871-3 *b*

Royal Army Medical Corps; C.M.G.

PORTER, Capt. H. J. A. ... ... 1875-7 *a*

The Devonshire Regt., 3rd Bn.; served from October 2nd, 1914, to June 1st, 1918; then retired.

*POTHECARY, Bt. Major W. F. ... 1895-9 *a*

The Hampshire Regiment, 5th Bn. (T.) (late Sergt., 1st Bn., London Rifle Brigade); seconded (1917) as Commandant, Southern Command Bombing School, Lyndhurst; D.C.M. (awarded when serving as Sergt. as above).

*POTT, Lieut. W. T. ... ... 1898-1903 *a*

9th (Queen's Royal) Lancers (Special Reserve); wounded, March 25th, 1918; M.C.

POUND, 2nd Lieut. J. V. ... 1912-17 *c*

Coldstream Guards, 4th Bn.

†POWELL, Lieut. E. L. ... ... 1909-13 *d*

Royal Field Artillery; served in France, for 18 months, with R.A.S.C., and then with 'B' Battery, 174th Brigade, 39th Division, and as Liaison Officer; killed at Cachy on April 6th, 1918.

*POWELL, Capt. (a./Major) H. S. ... 1907-11 *a*

Royal Flying Corps; mentioned in despatches; M.C.

POWELL, Rev. J. R. ... ... 1904-6 *a*

Army Chaplains' Department (attached 15th Bn., London Regiment, Civil Service Rifles).

POWELL, Pte. R. C. ... ... 1911-14 *a*

Honourable Artillery Company.

POWYS, Capt. A. R. ... ... 1895-9 *c*

Alexandra, Princess of Wales's Own Yorkshire Regiment, 2/4th Bn. (T.).

*POWYS, Sergt.-Major W. E. ... 1902-6 *c*

East African Service Corps; served in Bowker's Horse (East African Mounted Rifles) till disbanded; Croix de Chevalier de l' Ordre de Leopold II.

PRANCE, Lieut. G. B. S. ... 1910-14 *a*

Royal Field Artillery, 128th Howitzer Battery, 4th Division; gassed, September 23rd, 1917; discharged, due to wounds (gas), June 7th, 1918.

PREVOST, Cadet. E. J. ... ... 1915-18 *g*

Royal Navy; R.N.C., Keyham; attached H.M.S. Vivid.

*PREVOST, Lieut.-Col. G. H. ... 1883-6 *Price*

Indian Army; Commandant, 87th Punjabis; served in Mesopotamia; mentioned in despatches (twice).

PREVOST, Lieut. W. A. J. ... 1912-15 *g*

Royal Field Artillery, 401st Battery; served in France from September 14th, 1916; wounded.

PRIAULX, 2nd Lieut. O. ... ... 1913-17 *b*

Household Brigade, O.T.C., and 1st, and 3rd Bns., Scots Guards.

†PRICE, 2nd Lieut. E. W. M. ... 1911-14 *b*

The Hampshire Regiment, 3rd Bn. (Reserve); died in France of wounds received the same day, July 1st, 1916.

PRICHARD, Pioneer E. C. ... 1910-15 *f*

Royal Arsenal, Woolwich, and Bedford 'A' Signal Depôt, Royal Engineers.

†PRICHARD, Major R. G. M. ... 1890-4 *c*

1st Glamorgan Yeomanry (T.F.), attached Central India Horse, August, 1914; served in France; wounded there; March, 1918, went to Palestine and was there killed on June 7th, 1918.

*PRICHARD, Major W. O. ... 1892-7 *c*

The South Wales Borderers, 1st Bn.; wounded in France, 1914; mentioned in despatches.

PRINCE, Lieut. T. ... ... 1910-14 *a*

The Royal Sussex Regiment, 2nd Bn.; served in France.

PRITCHARD, Capt. H. T. ... 1881-2 *f*

Lincolnshire Yeomanry (T.F.); late King's Own Scottish Borderers.

PROSSER, Lieut. C. E. G. ... 1910-14 *d*

Royal Garrison Artillery (T.F.); discharged on account of ill-health, June 28th, 1918.

†PUCKRIDGE, Capt. C. F. H. ... 1908-12 *d*

The Duke of Cornwall's Light Infantry; served as Private in University and Public Schools' Corps, September 17th, 1914, to May 25th, 1915; Commissioned to 3rd Bn., D.C.L.I.; went to France September 19th, 1916, attached to 7th Bn.; promoted from 2nd Lieut. to Capt., September 19th, 1916; killed in action at Ruyaulcourt (between Bapaume and Cambrai), March 28th, 1917.

*PUCKRIDGE, Capt. H. V. ... 1911-15 *d*

The King's Shropshire Light Infantry; R.A.F.; taken prisoner, July 1st, 1918; released and landed in England, December 14th, 1918; D.F.C.

PUGH, Major H. O., D.S.O. ... 1888-9 *Price*
1st Welsh Horse, Yeomanry (T.F.); late Lumsden's Horse.

PUNCHARD, 2nd Lieut. C. ... 1911-14 *a*
Royal Field Artillery.

PUREFOY, Lieut. T. A. W. ... 1907-12 *c*
Royal Army Service Corps; attached West Yorkshire Regiment.

QUINEY, Lieut. R. C. ... ... 1911-14 *c*
Tank Corps, Depôt Bn., Wool; served in France with 16th Bn., The Duke of Cambridge's Own (Middlesex Regiment) and with 14th Bn., Tank Corps; twice wounded.

*RABAN, Brig.-Gen. Sir E., K.C.B. 1864-7 *a*
Royal Engineers; mentioned for War Service; K.B.E.

RADCLIFFE, Lieut. J. C. ... ... 1894-6 *c*
R.N.V.R.; Asst. Staff Officer to Rear Admiral, Stornoway, Isle of Lewis; formerly Ambulance driver, British Red Cross, Dunkirk, September, 1914, to June, 1915.

RADCLIFFE, 2nd Lieut. J. G. B. ... 1914-18 *a*
Devonshire Regiment, 3rd and 53rd Bns.

*RADCLIFFE, Lieut. W. H. ... 1907-12 a
The Devonshire Regiment, 2nd Bn.; served in France; mentioned in despatches (twice).

*RADCLYFFE, Capt. M. F. ... 1898-1901 *a*
4th (Queen's Own) Hussars; served in France with 10th Reserve Regt. of Cavalry from August 15th, 1914; twice wounded; mentioned in despatches (thrice); M.C.

RADCLYFFE, Lieut. R. A. ... ... 1905-7 *a*
4th (Royal Irish) Dragoon Guards; served in France from October 14th, 1915.

RADFORD, Lieut. A. D. ... ... 1888-94 *a*
The Devonshire Regiment, 11th (S.) Bn.

RAE, Commissioner E. V. R. ... 1904-9 *a*
Nigerian Land Contingent.

*RALEIGH, Lieut. A. G. ... ... 1911-15 *a*
The Leicestershire Regiment, 3rd Bn.; prisoner of war from March to December, 1918; M.C.

†RAMSAY, Lieut. D. W. ... ... 1905-9 *d*
The Sherwood Foresters (Nottinghamshire and Derbyshire Regiment), 10th (S.) Bn.; killed in the attack on the International Trench near Ypres, February 14th, 1916.

†RANSFORD, Capt. C. G. ... ... 1894-5 *a*
The South Staffordshire Regiment, 1st Bn.; went to Belgium with 7th Div. in October, 1914; three times wounded in an attack on a wood near Ypres on October 26th, 1914, and died next day in German hands.

RAWES, Capt. F. A. M. ... 1895-1900 *a*
Royal Air Force; served in France, in R.F.A., transferred to R.A.F., April, 1916; on Staff at Air Ministry for six months in 1918.

RAWLINS, Lieut. E. F. ... ... 1902-5 *f*
Indian Army; 10th Lancers; Indian Police.

RAY, 2nd Lieut. W. H. B. ... 1913-17 *a*

The Dorsetshire Regiment,6th Bn.; served in France; wounded at Thiepval.

†READ, Lieut. A. B. ... ... 1904-10 *f*

Prince Albert's (Somerset Light Infantry), 1st Bn.; went to France in August, 1914; killed at Crony in Battle of the Aisne, about September 19th, 1914.

REBBECK, Major T. V. ... ... 1901-5 *a*

The Hampshire Regiment, 1/7th Bn.(T.); served in Egypt from November, 1914, to 1919.

†REEVES, 2nd Lieut. L. ... ... 1913-17 *a*

The Hertfordshire Regiment, 1st Bn.; Commissioned, December, 1917; went to France, April, 1918; was gassed; attached 1st Bn., The Essex Regiment, in July, 1918; dangerously wounded in an attackon the 23rd, and died on the 25th August, 1918.

†REID-TAYLOR, Capt. A. A. C. ... 1889-94 *a*

The Royal Dublin Fusiliers; 1914, appointed Commandant at Port Said; Provost Marshall of Intelligence to General Staff; later sent to Indian Government to organise an Arab Force in Mesopotamia, at Basra; rejoined his Regiment at the Dardanelles, and was there killed on June 28th, 1915.

REES-WEBBE, 2nd Lieut. E. H. N. 1913-17 *b*

Royal Marine Artillery, Woolwich, and Royal Field Artillery.

RENTON, 2nd Lieut. M. J. ... 1912-18 *b*

Royal Marine Artillery, Woolwich, and 17th Battery, Royal Field Artillery.

*Renwick, Capt. A. E. ... ... 1912-14 *a*

Tank Corps ("F" Bn.); served as private in The London Regiment (London Scottish) till 1916; wounded November, 1917; M.C.

Reynell, Capt. G. M. ... 1897-1900 *a*

Royal Army Service Corps; Dep. Asst. Dir. of Supplies, Headquarters of Administrative Services and Departments.

†Richards, 2nd Lieut. J. D. E. ... 1899-1904 *T.*

The Royal Sussex Regiment, 2nd Bn.; at the outbreak of war he obtained a Commission in the Special Reserve; went to France, September, 1914, in R.E. Postal Section; transferred to Sussex Regiment in January, 1915; became Battalion M.G. Officer; killed at the Battle of Loos, September 25th, 1915.

Richmond, Capt. J. A. ... ... 1901-5 *b*

The South Staffordshire Regiment; served with 1st (Central Africa) Bn., King's African Rifles, 1914, to 1917; from 1918, at War Office.

*Rickett, Major G. R. ... ... 1911- *School M.O.*

R.A.M.C. (T.F.); attached Dorset Yeomanry; O.C., Nasiriya Military Hospital, Cairo; mentioned in despatches (twice); O.B.E.

Rickman, 2nd Lieut. J. ... ... 1887-93 *c*

Protectorate Forces, attached 1st Road Corps, East Africa.

*RICKMAN, Major (a./Lieut.-Col.) R. B. ... ... ... 1894-90 *f*

The Sherwood Foresters (Nottinghamshire and Derbyshire Regiment), 2/5th Bn. (T.); late Lieut., 3rd Cheshire Regiment; mentioned in despatches.

RIDOUT, Major C. A. S., M.S., M.B., Lond., F.R.C.S. Eng. ... ... 1887-94 *T.*

R.A.M.C. (T.F.); 5th Southern General Hospital, Portsmouth, 1914, to 1916; 29th Stationary Hospital, Salonika, 1916 to 1917; Italy, 1917 to 1918.

RIX, Capt. H. S. ... ... 1884-90 *a*

Indian Army; United Provinces Horse.

*ROBERTS, Capt. A. C. G. ... 1901-4 *d*

The Devonshire Regiment, 3rd, Bn.; attached 2nd Bn.; M.C.

†ROBERTSON, Lieut. W. M. ... 1906-10 *f*

The Lincolnshire Regiment, 2nd Bn.; went to France, August, 1914, as 2nd Lieut.; wounded, August 26th; made Lieut. in December; wounded again on January 24th, 1915, when with 2nd Bn.; killed at Bois Grenier, near Armentières, June 27th, 1915.

†ROBINSON, 2nd Lieut. B. S. ... 1910-13 *d*

Princess Charlotte of Wales's (Royal Berkshire Regiment), 2nd Bn.; passed out of Sandhurst in May, 1915; promoted 1st Lieut. in November, 1915; killed in action near Albert, France, July 1st, 1916.

ROBINSON, Major F. H., M.B., B.C. 1899-1903 *b*

R.A.M.C., 'A' Force.

ROBINSON, Lieut. R. G. ... ... 1910-14 *c*

Machine Gun Corps, 49th Bn.; wounded at Bourlon Wood, November 23rd, 1917; previously served in 13th, 20th and 14th Bns., The Welsh Regiment, and 121st Machine Gun Company.

ROBINSON, Lieut. S. G. ... ... 1913-15 *c*

Royal Air Force.

ROGERS, Lieut. H. ... ... 1912-14 *a*

Royal Garrison Artillery; 182nd Siege Battery.

*ROGERSON, Major E. C. ... ... 1884-7 *b*

Royal Garrison Artillery; served in France, 1915, to 1917; mentioned in despatches.

*ROMER, Lieut.-Col. F., M.D. ... 1884-9 *a*

R.A.M.C.; served in Gallipoli campaign; mentioned for War Services, 1917; invalided out on account of injuries received on active service, December, 1918.

ROMER, Lieut. R. P. ... ... 1910-14 *a*

Royal Air Force; from October 19th, 1914, to June 18th, 1915, was in 9th (S.) Bn., The Royal Dublin Fusiliers.

*ROOM, Capt. L. C. T. ... ... 1897-1901 *c*

Royal Marines; served in Gallipoli; mentioned in despatches.

ROPER, Capt. J. ... ... 1900-4 *a*

The Dorsetshire Regiment, 1/4th Bn. (T.); served in India.

†ROSE, 2nd Lieut. H. P.... ... 1911-15 *f*

Seaforth Highlanders (Ross-shire Buffs, The Duke of Albany's), 2nd Bn.; passed out of Sandhurst, January, 1916; went to France, October, 1916; killed in action at the Battle of Arras, near Fampoux, April 11th, 1917.

†ROSS, 2nd Lieut. R. C. ... ... 1909-12 *b*

The Royal Scots (Lothian Regiment), 2nd Bn.; missing, presumed killed, August 26th, 1914, in France.

ROUQUETTE, Lieut. L. P. ... 1911-15 *a*

Indian Army; 39th Mountain Battery, Indian Expeditionary Force.

ROXBY, 2nd Lieut. N. E. M. ... 1895-9 *T.*

Royal Army Service Corps.

RULE, 2nd Lieut. F. G. ... ... 1914-18 *d*

Royal Engineers.

*RUSSELL, Capt. G. B. ... ... 1910-14 *d*

The Duke of Edinburgh's (Wiltshire Regiment), 1st Bn.; attached 3rd Bn.; D.S.O.

RUSSELL, 2nd Lieut. J. N. ... 1913-18 *a*

The Royal Fusiliers (City of London Regiment), 3rd Garrison Bn.

†RUSSELL, 2nd Lieut. P. A. ... 1903-7 *b*

Lovatt's Scouts; attached Royal Air Force; killed, April 2nd, 1917, in France.

†RUTHERFURD, Pte. H. G. G. ... 1902-5 *f*

The Royal Fusiliers (City of London Regiment), 10th Bn.; went to France, July, 1915; killed in advance on Pozieres, June, 1916.

RYBOT, 2nd Lieut. F. J. C. ... 1915-17 *c*
Royal Garrison Artillery.

*SALMON, Lieut.-Col. G. N. ... 1885-9 *b*
The Rifle Brigade (The Prince Consort's Own), 4th Bn.; mentioned in despatches (four times); C.M.G.; D.S.O.; Distinguished Service Medal (America).

SAMLER, Capt. W. H. G. ... 1909-13 *a*
Prince Albert's (Somerset Light Infantry), 1/4th Bn. (T.); served in Mesopotamia, Egypt and Salonika.

SAMUELSON, Capt. G. S. ... ... 1880-3 *Price*
R.A.M.C.; late Capt. Australian A.M.C.

SANCTUARY, Lieut. A. G. E. ... 1904-10 *a*
Royal Field Artillery; 1st Dorsetshire Battery, 3rd Wessex Brigade (T.); served in Mesopotamia.

SANCTUARY, Capt. C. T. ... ... 1902-8 *a*
Royal Field Artillery; attached Royal Air Force.

†*SANDERS, Capt. A. E. ... ... 1904-10 *T.*
The York and Lancaster Regiment, 2nd Bn.; went to France, December, 1914; gazetted Capt. early in 1915; served throughout in Ypres salient; mentioned in despatches; died of wounds received on May 19th, 1916.

SANDERS, Capt. E. A. ... ... 1904-10 *T.*
The Dorsetshire Regiment, 5th (S.) Bn., attached 7th (S.) Bn.

SANDERS, W. R. ... ... 1904-8 *T.*
London Regiment, 2/17th Bn.

†Sawyer, Capt. R. H. ... ... 1906-8 *b*

Royal Air Force; enlisted in Canada; chosen for a Commission and attached to Artists' Rifles on arriving in England; joined 36th Squadron as a night Pilot on Home Defence; was C.O. at Hylton and Ashington; went to France in February, 1918, in the 100th Squadron—independent Air Force; died on leave, in London, on August 3rd, 1918, of illness.

Saxon Capt. (a./Major) E. ... 1906-11 *f*

Royal Field Artillery; 3rd Cheshire Battery, The Cheshire Brigade (T.); served in France, Egypt and Mesopotamia, with various units; promoted a./Major while commanding 75th Battery, R.F.A., November, 1918, to January, 1919.

*Saxon, Capt. H. ... ... 1895-99 *f*

The Royal Sussex Regiment; served in France, in the ranks, with the Royal Fusiliers, and, when commissioned, with 9th Bn., Royal Sussex Regiment; Prisoner of War, March 22nd, 1918; M.C.

†*Sayres, Lieut.-Col. A. W. F., M.R.C.S., L.R.C.P. ... ... ... 1882-4 *Price*

R.A.M.C. (T.F.); was in Camp on outbreak of war and volunteering for foreign service went to France as Major of 1st Wessex Field Ambulance (later called 24th) on November 5th, 1914; made Lieut.-Col., January, 1916, in Command of 2/1st Wessex; mentioned in despatches; severely wounded by a shell in the trenches on July 17th, 1917, and died of his wounds on October, 10th, 1917.

†Scarbrough, Capt. R. J. ... 1894-98 *a*

Devonshire Regiment, 3rd Bn.; at outbreak of war joined Indian Army Reserve of Officers on Garrison work in India; came to England, August, 1915; rejoined Devons as Capt., September, 1915; sailed for Egypt, November, 1916; was attached to 8th Bn., Hampshire Regiment; wounded at Gaza; died in Palestine, November 2nd, 1917.

Scobell, Capt. W. B. ... ... 1901-5 *a*

Royal Berkshire Regiment.

Scott, Col. B. ... ... ... 1877-8 *a*

Indian Army.

Scott, Col. C. D. ... ... 1874-7 *a*

Royal Garrison Artillery; Chief Instructor in Gunnery, Coast Defences, Scottish (East).

Scott, 2nd Lieut. T. A. R. ... 1913-16 *g*

Royal Engineers.

Scott, 2nd Lieut. G. C. ... 1911-16 *f*

Royal Field Artillery, A/246 Battery.

Scott, 2nd Lieut. S. ... ... 1912-15 *c*

Prince Albert's (Somerset Light Infantry), attached 3rd Bn.

Scott, Major W. G. ... ... 1900-2 *c*

Devonshire Regiment, 2nd Bn., and 284th Machine Gun Coy.; wounded in France; also served in India (N.W.F.).

†Scott-Holmes, Lieut. B. ... 1897-1901 *a*

The King's Royal Rifle Corps, 16th (S.) Bn. (C.L.B.); killed in motor accident at Wandsworth.

SHARLAND, Gunner W. S. C. ... 1905-7 *d*
Australian Field Artillery.

*SHARP, Capt. A. ... ... 1901-3 *b*
Canadian Expeditionary Force; 19th Alberta Dragoons and Canadian Light Horse; served in France; M.C.

SHARP, Lieut. H. A. ... ... 1902-3 *a*
The Royal West Surrey (Queen's) Regiment, 9th (Reserve) Bn., in Salonika; transferred to 8th King's Shropshire Light Infantry; wounded and invalided home through shell shock.

SHAW, Capt. H. E. ... ... 1894-7 *f*
Royal Air Force; served in France with 7th (S.) Bn., The Rifle Brigade (The Prince Consort's Own); invalided out, June, 1916; Lieut., R.N.V.R., August 26th, 1916; Capt., R.A.F., April, 1918.

SHAW, Lieut. N. L. ... ... 1905-9 *a*
2nd King Edward's Horse (The King's Oversea Dominions Regiment); served in France.

†SHAW, Lieut. W. E. ... ... 1902-7 *f*
The King's Shropshire Light Infantry, 2nd Bn.; died, May 31st, of wounds received on March 15th, 1915.

SHEARS, Capt. R. H. ... ... 1907-11 *f*
The King's Shropshire Light Infantry, 1st Bn.; and Royal Air Force; served in India.

SHETTLE, Lieut.-Col. H. W. ... 1869-74 *Price*
R.A.M.C. (T.F.); Medical Officer, Red Cross Hospital, Highfield Hall, Southampton; died, April, 1919.

SHEWELL, Capt. A. V. ... ... 1911-13 *c*

The Gloucestershire Regiment, seconded to R.A.F.; served in France; wounded in air fight, November 17th, 1916; on London Defence since October, 1917.

†SHIPPARD, Pte. C. N. W. ... 1905-7 *a*

1st New Zealand Expeditionary Force; joined Wellington Infantry Bn., August, 1914; landed at Gallipoli, April 25th, 1915; transferred to M. G. Corps; wounded, and sent home; went to France and was killed at Armentières, July 10th, 1916.

SIMEY, Rifleman P. A. T. ... 1907-11 *f*

North Rhodesia Rifles, Rhodesia; Assist. Commissioner and Justice of Peace for North Rhodesia.

†SIMMONS, Capt. F. W. ... ... 1901-6 *f*

The Hampshire Regiment; August, 1914, joined the O.T.C. Camp, Salisbury Plain, and was commissioned to 2/4th Bn. (T.), Hants Regiment; December, 1914, went to India with his Bn.; September, 1915, promoted Captain at Quetta; April, 1919, went to Egypt, and then to Palestine; killed at Nebi Samuil (Mizpah) on November 22nd, 1917, in attack on Jerusalem, having been previously wounded earlier in the day.

†SIMMONS, Capt. P. E. M. ... 1907-12 *f*

The Hampshire Regiment, 1/4th Bn. (T.); August, 1914, was in Camp with his Bn. as 1st Lieut.; promoted Capt.; October, 1914, went to India with his Bn.; March, 1915, went to Mesopotamia with his Bn., and was killed in attack on Nasiriyeh on July 24th, 1915.

Simmons, 2nd Lieut. V. A. ... 1913-17 *f*
The Hampshire Regiment, 4th Bn.

Simonds, 2nd Lieut. R. M. H. ... 1912-16 *a*
Royal Garrison Artillery.

Simpson, Lieut. B. Z. ... ... 1911-15 *a*
Royal Air Force; equipment officer.

†*Slade, Major R. B. ... ... 1906-8 *d*
Royal Garrison Artillery; joined No. 1 Company, Poole, Dorsetshire (T.), in August, 1914; went to France and was transferred to 123rd Siege Battery; mentioned in despatches, 1917; killed in France on July 10th, 1918.

†Slater, Lieut. T. A. F. ... 1909-13 *d*
The Dorsetshire Regiment, 5th Bn.; missing, presumed killed, between September 25th, 26th, 1916, at Thiepval Ridge.

*Sloman, Brig.-Genl. H. S., D.S.O. 1876-9 *f*
mentioned for War Services and in despatches (twice); C.M.G.; Order of Sacred Treasure.

Smallwood, Lieut. G. Le W. ... 1886-9 *a*
Royal Field Artillery (Special Reserve); 1st Bn. Reserve Brigade, R.F.A.; served in France, with 38th Division.

†Smith, Capt. D. G. ... ... 1905-9 *a*
Royal Engineers; died of wounds in France, June 26th, 1916.

Smith, Brig.-Gen. G. B. ... 1872-7 *f*
Inspector of R.H. and F.A. in India; Technical Adviser to O.C. Expeditionary Force in Mesopotamia.

SMITH, Capt. G. W. Melson ... 1903-7 *c*

Head Quarters, Claims Commission, British Expeditionary Force, June, 1916, to September, 1919.

*SMITH, Bt. Lieut.-Col. H.M., D.S.O. 1884-7 *a*

The King's Shropshire Light Infantry; Commanding 5th (S.) Bn.; mentioned in despatches.

SMITH, Major J. U. ... ... 1903-7 *f*

Royal Field Artillery; 2/4th East Anglian Brigade, 2/2nd Hertfordshire Battery (T.).

†SMITH, 2nd Lieut. L. S. ... 1910-14 *f*

The Wiltshire Regiment, 1st Bn.; in August, 1914, joined Honourable Artillery Co., as private; September 18th, 1914, went to France as signaller with 1st Bn., H.A.C.; January 19th, 1915, given a Commission (in France) in 2nd South Lancashires; April, 1915, transferred to 1st Bn., Wilts Regiment; killed accidentally by a hand-grenade, near Ypres, June 13th, 1915.

*SMITH, Capt. N. H. ... ... 1905-7 *d*

R.A.M.C.; served with North Russian Expeditionary Force; Croix de Guerre.

*SMITH, Capt. P. ... ... 1898-1903 *f*

R.A.M.C.; Medical Officer, 2nd Irish Guards; severely wounded, November, 1916; mentioned in despatches (twice); M.C.

SMITH, Rifleman R. S. ... ... 1911-13 *f*

16th County of London Regiment, Queen's Westminster Rifles; also served with 1st and 3rd Bn. in France.

†**Smith**, Capt. V. N. ... ... 1896-8 *c*

Wiltshire Regiment (The Duke of Edinburgh's), 6th Bn.; given Commission at outbreak of war in Wilts Regiment; March, 1915, promoted Capt.; July, 1915, went to France; October, 1915, wounded; February, 1916, returned to France; killed in Regina Trench, before Miraumonte, France, November 13th, 1916.

**Smyth**, A. J. ... ... ... 1910-14 *b*

Civilian Prisoner; a member of the School, spending holidays in Heidelberg; interned at Ruhleben, November 6th, 1914, to 1918.

†**Smyth**, Capt. W. H. ... ... 1892-6 *a*

The Devonshire Regiment; Commissioned to 11th (S.) Bn., Devons, November, 1914; January, 1916; transferred unfit for active service to 1st Garrison Battalion The Worcestershire Regiment as Musketry Officer; November, 1917, went to France with 2nd Bn., Worcesters; killed in action at Neuve Eglise, April 17th, 1918.

***Sopper**, Bt. Major (temp. Lieut.-Col.) F. W. ... ... ... 1893-8 *f*

18th (Queen Mary's Own) Hussars; mentioned in despatches (thrice), and for war services.

**Southey**, Pte. C. S. ... ... 1906-7 *f*

R.A.M.C.; 27th Field Ambulance, 9th Division, B.E.F.

**Sparks**, 2nd Lieut. A. B. ... 1914-17 *g*

Royal Air Force.

SPENCER, Lieut. J. H. ... ... 1912-16 *a*

The Dorsetshire Regiment, 2nd Bn.; served with Egyptian Expeditionary Force, Palestine, October, 1917, to March, 1919; in India from October, 1919.

SPREADBURY, 2nd Lieut. H. J. H. 1912-15 *c*

Tank Corps.

SPROULE, Lieut. E. R. L. ... 1914-16 *d*

Royal Naval Air Service and Royal Air Force; wounded, September 4th, 1918; prisoner of war in Germany, from that date; reached England, January 5th, 1919.

†*SPURWAY, Lieut. G. V. ... ... 1907-10 *c*

Prince Albert's (Somerset Light Infantry), 9th (S.) Bn.; joined Sportsman's Bn., October, 1914; Commissioned to S.L.I., 1915; transferred to M.G. Corps; went to France, August, 1916, with 167th M.G. Coy.; M.C.; killed in the abortive German attack on Arras on March 28th, 1918.

†SPURWAY, 2nd Lieut. R. P. ... 1904-9 *c*

Prince Albert's (Somerset Light Infantry), 9th (S.) Bn.; attached to 2nd Bn., Hampshire Regiment, December, 1914; despatched in August, 1915, to Gallipoli on the Royal Edward, and was drowned when that ship was torpedoed on August 14th, 1915.

*SQUARE, Major A. H. ... ... 1901-3 *c*

Royal Field Artillery; mentioned in despatches; M.C.

†STACKE, Lieut. O. G. N. ... 1909-12 *c*

The Royal Inniskilling Fusiliers, 2nd Bn.; killed in France, 1915.

†STALEY, Lieut. F. C. ... ... 1903-8 *b*

Prince Albert's (Somerset Light Infantry), 5th Bn.(T.); killed in Mesopotamia, March 8th, 1916.

STALLARD, Lieut. G. W. ... 1913-17 *a*

Royal Air Force.

*STANFORD, Lieut. E. J. ... ... 1913-16 *f*

The Wiltshire Regiment, 4th Bn.; served in France with 7th Bn.; wounded and awarded M.C., October 18th, 1918.

*STANGER-LEATHES, Major H. E. ... 1891-6 *d*

Indian Medical Service; served in Mesopotamia; mentioned in despatches; October, 1918, appointed Deputy Asst. Director Medical Services, Southern Command, Poona.

STARK, 2nd Lieut. M. A. N. W. ... 1911-15 *f*

The King's Shropshire Light Infantry, 9th (S.) Bn., and 11th Leicesters.

STARK, 2nd Lieut. R. G. W. ... 1906-8 *f*

The King's Shropshire Light Infantry, 5th (S.) Bn.

*STEPHENS, Major F. A. ... ... 1885-8 *Price*

R.A.M.C.; served in France, 1914 and 1915; in Macedonia, 1916 to 1919; mentioned in despatches; D.S.O.; Order of Saint Sava (Serbian).

STEPHENS, Major J. A., T.D. ... 1885-7 *Price*

Royal Field Artillery, 2nd Dorsetshire Battery, 3rd Wessex Brigade (T.); invalided out in January, 1918, on account of ill-health contracted on active service.

STEVENS, Lieut.-Col. A. F. ... 1885-6 *f*
Indian Medical Service; Divisional S.M.O., 6th Poona Division.

†*STEVENSON, Lieut. L. W. H. ... 1910-14 *b*
The Royal Inniskilling Fusiliers, 9th (S.) Bn. (Co. Tyrone); M.C.; killed, in the battle of the Somme, at Thiepval, July 1st, 1916.

STEWARD, Lieut. J. R. O'B. ... 1911-14 *g*
1/1 Lincolnshire Yeomanry (T.F.)

STEWART, (temp. Capt.) E. W. Hylton 1901-5 *a*
Canadian Army Service Corps; 4th Canadian Divisional Train; served in France and Belgium.

*STICKNEY, Major J. E. D. ... 1895-8 *d*
The York and Lancaster Regiment, 2/4th Bn.; mentioned in despatches; D.S.O.; M.C. with one bar.

STILLWELL, Lieut. C. D. ... 1896-8 *f*
Royal Army Service Corps; 36th (Ulster) Divisional M.T. Company.

*STOCKTON, Lieut. B. H. B. ... 1912-16 *a*
Royal Field Artillery; served with A/75th Brigade, with Guards' Division, from November, 1917; afterwards in the Northern Division, B.A.O., Germany; mentioned in despatches; M.C.

STOCKTON, Lieut. H. O. ... ... 1908-11 *c*
The Oxfordshire and Buckinghamshire Light Infantry, 3/4th Bn. (T.).

STONE, 2nd Lieut. G. F. J. P. ... 1913-16 *c*
The Devonshire Regiment, 3rd Bn.

STORRS, Capt. K. S., M.B. (T.F.) ... 1882-5 *a*
R.A.M.C.; attached 5th (T.) Bn., Essex Regiment.

STOTESBURY, Lieut. A. M. ... 1912-16 *b*
Gloucestershire Regiment.

STRANGMAN, Lieut. H. W. ... 1903-7 *c*
Royal Field Artillery; 167th Anti-Aircraft Section, Independent Force, R.A.F.

†STREATFIELD, 2nd Lieut. T. B. M. 1911-16 *a*
The Queen's Own (Royal West Kent Regiment); November, 1916, entered Sandhurst; September, 1917, gazetted to Royal West Kent Regiment, 1st Bn., and went to France; killed in action near Passchendaele, November 7th, 1917.

*STREET, Major (temp. Lieut.-Col.) A. 1885-91 *b*
Royal Army Service Corps; O.B.E.

*STROUD, Col. (temp. Brig.-Gen.) E. J. 1880-6 *Price*
Royal Marine Light Infantry; Commandant Plymouth Division; commanded 1st Bn. in Gallipoli; commanded 2nd Brigade, Royal Naval Division at the evacuation of Gallipoli and, subsequently, in Salonika and in France; commanded troops in Aegean Islands, 1917, to July, 1918; Military Governor of Lemnos, Imbros and Tenedos; mentioned in despatches (twice); C.M.G.

STRUCKMEYER, O. K. ... ... 1907-12 *f*
Civilian Prisoner; interned at Ruhleben from November, 1914, to November, 1918.

STUART-PRINCE, Capt. D. ... 1909-14 *a*

Indian Army, Reserve of Officers; attached Indian Munitions Board.

*STUDD, Capt. T. Q. ... ... 1906-7 *d*

Royal Flying Corps; D.F.C.

*SUNDERLAND, Major B. G. E. 1896-1900 *a*

Royal Garrison Artillery; twice mentioned for war services; O.B.E.; Cavalier Order of St. Maurice.

†SWABEY, 2nd Lieut. A. M. C. ... 1909-13 *b*

Prince Albert's (Somerset Light Infantry), 3rd Bn.; killed, near Zonnebeke, April 20th, 1915.

SWANWICK, E. D. ... ... 1884-90 *f*

Guards Officer Cadet Battalion.

SWEET, Rev. G. C. W. ... ... 1904-9 *a*

Chaplain to the Forces in France, 1918-19.

†SWEET, Capt. L. H. ... ... 1908-11 *a*

In Expeditionary Force, August, 1914; at Le Cateau; joined R.F.C., December, 1914; Flight Commander (temp. Capt.), February, 1916; killed in air combat, June 22nd, in Belgium.

*SYMES, Capt. (a./Major) A. L. ... 1904-7 *b*

Royal Field Artillery; 1/1st Devonshire Battery, 4th Wessex Brigade (T.); served in India, September, 1914, to August, 1916; then in Mesopotamia with 14th Battery, 4th Brigade, R.F.A., 3rd Division, till April, 1918; afterwards in Palestine and Egypt with 'A' Battery, 302nd Brigade, R.F.A., 60th Division; mentioned in despatches.

Symes, Pte. W. E. ... ... 1907-8 *a*

Royal Garrison Artillery, 2nd Heavy Brigade; and 448th Agriculture Coy., Exeter.

*Symonds, Capt. H. S. P. ... 1903-7 *a*

The London Regiment, 1/7th (City of London) Bn.; served in France; twice wounded; February, 1919, Adjutant 7th (Reserve) Bn., The London Regiment; mentioned for war services.

†Symons, Pte. H. N. ... ... 1904-5 *d*

1/13th (Kensingtons) London Regiment, and Divisional Train of the 56th (London) Division; served in France continuously from October, 1914, until killed in action, near Arras, on December 6th, 1917.

Tamplin, Col. H. T., C.M.G., K.C., J.P. ... ... ... 1863-9 *a*

(Ret. South African Defence Forces); Inns of Court Reserve; commanded Fleet Street Volunteers, subsequently merged into City of London Brigade.

*Tancock, Lieut.-Col. O. K. ... 1877-80 *c*

Indian Army; Indian Mountain Batteries; Commandant 27th Mountain Battery; C.M.G.

*Tayler, Lieut. (a./Capt.) J. R. ... 1905-9 *c*

The Duke of Edinburgh's (Wiltshire Regiment), 3rd Bn.; mentioned in despatches (twice); M.C.

Tayler, 2nd Lieut. R. ... ... 1908-11 *c*

The Dorsetshire Regiment, 3rd Bn.

Tayler, Lieut. S. E. ... ... 1912-15 *a*

Indian Army; 2/39th Garhwal Rifles.

TAYLOR, Rev. A. C. ... ... 1863-4 *b*

Senior Chaplain (retired) Government of India.

TAYLOR, Pte. F. Sherwood ... 1911-16 *g*

Honourable Artillery Company; wounded in France and discharged unfit, December, 1918.

TAYLOR, Capt. H. H. C. R.

(see REID-TAYLOR).

TAYLOR, Major, The Rev. R. B., D.D. ... ... ... 1884-7 *d*

Canadian Expeditionary Force; 42nd Bn. (Royal Highlanders of Canada); now Principal of Queen's University, Kingston, Ontario.

*TEMPERLEY, Bt. Lieut.-Col. A. C. 1891-6 *a*

The Norfolk Regiment; G.S.O. (1), Fifth Army; mentioned in despatches (four times; C.M.G.; D.S.O.

*TEMPERLEY, Major H. W. V. ... 1893-8 *b*

2nd Fife and Forfar Yeomanry (T.F.); G.S.O. (2); Order of Crown of Roumania; Order of Kora George; Assistant Military Attaché, Serbian Army; O.B.E.

TERRY, Major H. C. E. ... ... 1904-9 *d*

Royal Field Artillery; wounded, June, 1917.

†TERRY, Lieut. J. E. ... ... 1904-8 *d*

Royal Flying Corps; died of blood poisoning, at Rouen, October 17th, 1917.

TESTER, 2nd Lieut. A. F. ... 1903- *Master*
The Queen's Own (Royal West Kent Regiment), 1/4th Bn. (T.); attached General Staff, India.

THATCHER, Capt. A. F. B. ... 1911-14 *f*
Prince Albert's (Somerset Light Infantry), 2/4th Bn. (T.); attached to 1/10th Gurkha Rifles.

THOMAS, Lieut.-Col. A. E. ... 1858-62 *a*
Late 7th Dragoon Guards.

THOMAS, Surgeon E. J. F. 1899-1900 *d*
H.M.S. 'Brilliant.'

THOMAS, Gentleman Cadet P. H. ... 1912-15 *d*
Royal Military College, Sandhurst; invalided out through ill-health.

*THOMAS, Capt. R. C. ... 1898-1902 *c*
Royal Engineers; M.C.

THORNTON, 2nd Lieut. G. K. ... 1912-17 *b*
Royal Field Artillery, 14th (Res.) Battery.

THORNTON, Midshipman R. H. ... 1914-17 *b*
Royal Navy.

*THURSTON, Lieut.-Col. V. B. ... 1891-5 *d*
The Dorsetshire Regiment; served in Cameroon Campaign to May, 1916; commanded 9th Bn., The Lancashire Fusiliers, in France, October, 1916, to November, 1917; invalided; commanding 4th Bn. (T.), The Dorsetshire Regiment; mentioned in despatches (thrice).

TODD, Major A. H. ... ... 1900-3 *f*

Royal Air Force (Medical Service); O.C. of the R.A.F. Hospital, Blandford.

TODD, Lieut. C. L. ... ... 1911-14 *f*

The Dorsetshire Regiment, 6th (S.) Bn.

TODD-JONES, 2nd Lieut. G. B. ... 1912-16 *a*

Royal Field Artillery; B/232nd Army Brigade.

TOOGOOD, 2nd Lieut. H. C. ... 1911-14 *b*

The Norfolk Regiment, 1st Bn.

TORDIFFE, Capt. H. S. W. ... 1881-9 *a*

The Duke of Edinburgh's (Wiltshire Regiment) (Reserve of Officers).

TOWNSEND, 2nd Lieut. P. D. ... 1906-9 *a*

Royal Field Artillery, 2 B. Reserve Brigade, Special Reserve.

*TOZER (a./Capt.) A. ... ... 1906-11 *a*

Royal Engineers (Signal Service), attached to O.C. Signal Section, 17th Corps Heavy Artillery; M.C.

TOZER, Capt. G. A. ... ... 1893-5 *a*

The London Regiment, 8th (City of London) Bn. (Post Office Rifles); Adjutant 8th (Reserve) Bn., April, 1915, to September, 1917; Assistant Controller, attached to American Tank Commission, September, 1917, to February, 1919.

*TOZER, Major J. C. ... ... 1904-7 *a*

Royal Army Ordnance Corps; mentioned in H.S. despatches.

†TRASK, Lieut. C. W. T. ... ... 1913-16 *a*

Prince Albert's (Somerset Light Infantry); attached to The Welsh Regiment; served in Egypt and Palestine; killed on Western Front, August 18th, 1918.

TRELAWNY-ROSS, Lieut. A. H. { 1899-1905 *a* / 1911- *Master* }

Unattached List (T.F.), Sherborne O.T.C.

TRELAWNY-ROSS, Pte. S. M. T. ... 1909-13 *b*

Artists' Rifles, 1/28th (County of London) Bn.; prisoner of war, in Bayreuth, Bavaria, March 24th, to December 12th, 1918.

*TRELAWNY-ROSS, Rev. W.T., C.F. 1898-1903 *a*

The Royal Fusiliers (City of London Regiment), 26th Bn.; served in France; M.C.

TREMAINE, Lieut.-Col. R. ... 1874-6 *c*

Royal Garrison Artillery (Res. of Officers).

TREVOR, Capt. C. P. ... ... 1904-8 *c*

King's Liverpool Regiment, 2nd Bn.; served on N.W. Frontier, India, 1914, to 1915; Mesopotamia, 1916, and France, 1917; 2nd in Command and Temporary O.C., 12th Bn., The King's Regiment, in France; also served with 20th Divisional Staff; left France, February, 1918, for India, and served with 2/2nd Gurkhas, N.W.F.; commanded column on Kuki operations, Burma, in January, 1919.

TRUEMAN, Coy. Sergt.-Major T. L. 1906-10 *a*

Volunteer Calcutta Rifles, 1st Bn.; invalided out.

†TUCKER, 2nd Lieut. A. R. L. ... 1910-12 *c*

The Royal Warwickshire Regiment, 2nd Bn. (from Unattached List, I.A.); killed between Fleurbaix and Le Mesnil, December 18th, 1914.

TUCKER, Capt. J. A. C. ... ... 1904-5 *a*

The Dorsetshire Regiment, 1/4th Bn. (T.); served in Mesopotamia; wounded.

TUCKER, Lieut.-Col. (Hon. Col.) R. E. V.D. ... ... ... 1877-81 *c*

The Devonshire Regiment, 2/5th Bn. (T.); September, 1915, to July, 1916, on active service in Egypt; October, 1916, to March, 1917, commanded 66th Provisional Bn.; June, 1917, to May, 1918, Staff appointment with B.E.F., France.

TUKE, 2nd Lieut. A. F. M. ... 1909-13 *c*

Royal Field Artillery; served from 1915, to 1917, in Ceylon Planters' Rifle Corps; from April, 1918, in France, in 'A' Battery, 160th Brigade, R.F.A.

†TUKE, 2nd Lieut. A. H. S. ... 1904-10 *c*

The Northumberland Fusiliers, 3rd Bn.; killed, near Ypres, May 7th, 1915.

TULLIS, Capt, G. D. ... ... 1905-7 *c*

R.A.M.C.; joined as temp. Lieut., December, 1915; Capt., December, 1916; served with 23rd Division in France and Flanders and with No. 50 Casualty Clearing Station; demobilised, December, 1918.

*TURNER, Major W. A. ... ... 1894-8 *d*

The King's (Liverpool Regiment), 6th (Rifle) Bn. (T.); mentioned in despatches.

†TURRELL, 2nd Lieut. H. G. ... 1911-13 *c*
The Oxfordshire and Buckinghamshire Light Infantry; wounded, near Passchendaele, August 22nd, 1917; died at St. Thomas' Hospital, November 3rd, 1917.

TURTON, Capt. L. N. ... ... 1883-86 *Prep.*
Royal Navy.

*TURTON, Major M. S. ... ... 1887-92 *T.*
Royal Army Ordnance Department; D.A.D.O.S., 14th Division, Mesopotamia; served in France, Mesopotamia and Persia; mentioned in despatches.

TUSON, Fleet Paymaster (Ret.) A. K. 1862-6 *a*
Additional President for the South of Ireland Coast Guard.

TWEEDY, Major A. C., T.D. ... 1880-3 *c*
Royal Garrison Artillery (T.).

TYSON, Cadet D. ... ... 1914-16 *Prep.*
Royal Navy: 1917, Osborne; 1919, Dartmouth.

VACHELL, Lieut.-Col. H. R. ... 1866-70 *c*
Royal Army Medical Corps (T.F.).

†VACHER, 2nd Lieut. G. H. ... 1908-13 *c*
The Royal Warwickshire Regiment, 2nd Bn.; killed at or near Zandvoorde, on or about October 31st, 1914.

VACHER, 2nd Lieut. W. E. ... 1910-14 *c*
The Duke of Edinburgh's (Wiltshire Regiment), 7th (S.) Bn.

VAN DER BŸL, Capt. A. L. M. ... 1908-11 *a*

Cape Garrison Artillery; Sectional Commander German West Africa Campaign; served in France with R.F.A., 1915; transferred to R.A.F., 1917; Examining Officer, 18th Wing, R.A.F., Headquarters, London.

†VAN GOETHEM, Capt. and Flight-Commander H. E. ... ... 1908-11 *a*

Royal Flying Corps, 10th Squadron; seriously wounded in an aeroplane accident, May 5th, 1916; Instructor to Beaulieu Aerodrome, July 5th, 1917; killed while instructing a junior officer in flying, July 11th, 1917.

*VAN STRAUBENZEE, Brig.-Gen., C. H. C. ... ... ... 1879-81 *d*

Mentioned in despatches (twice); C.B.; C.M.G.; C.B.E.

VEALE, Lieut. A. P. ... ... 1904-7 *a*

Royal Engineers, 177th Tunnelling Company; formerly in 184th Company.

VENNING, Capt. E. G. ... 1898-1904 *f*

The Duke of Cornwall's Light Infantry, 1/4th Bn. (T.); served in Egypt.

VERNON, Lieut. A. S. ... ... 1913-15 *g*

Royal Army Service Corps; Siege Park, Rhine Army, Cologne.

VERNON, Major J. B. ... 1899-1900 *b*

Royal Air Force; Vice-Consul at Dunkirk.

†VICARY, Capt. G. D. ... ... 1902-3 *d*

The Devonshire Regiment, 5th Bn. (T.); died in Palestine, November 10th, of wounds received November 8th, 1917.

*VICARY, Lieut. J. ... ... 1909-11 *d*

The Gloucestershire Regiment, 2nd Bn.; mentioned in despatches (thrice); M.C. and two bars.

*VILLAR, Capt. P. L. ... ... 1904-6 *b*

The South Wales Borderers, 7th (S.) Bn.; mentioned in despatches; M.C.

VINCENT, a./Sergt. J. ... ... 1908-9 *b*

Royal Engineers, despatch rider; also served in 13th Corps Signal Company (Canadian).

†Vincent, Capt. W. ... ... 1878-82 *a*

The Duke of Cornwall's Light Infantry, 3rd Bn. (Reserve); attached to 1st Bn., Royal Welsh Fusiliers; killed during the retreat from Mons, 1914.

†*VINTER, 2nd Lieut. R. B. W. ... 1909-14 *b*

The Worcestershire Regiment, 6th Bn. (Reserve); M.C.; killed, October 30th, 1916, between Lesboeufs and Morval.

†*VIZARD, Capt. H. T. ... ... 1910-14 *T.*

Royal Field Artillery, 15th Division (Scottish); mentioned in despatches (five times); M.C. with two bars; killed, September 1st, 1918, near Arras, by a splinter from bomb dropped by aeroplane.

VOSPER, Lieut. D. ... ... 1907-11 *a*

The Suffolk Regiment, 4th Bn.; transferred to 247th P.O.W. Company; served in Gallipoli, Egypt and France.

†VOWLER, Capt. (temp. Major) D.F.S. 1910-12 *a*
Nottinghamshire and Derbyshire Regiment, and Machine Gun Corps; died, February 28th, 1919, of pneumonia contracted in Camp at Hazeley Down, Winchester.

VOWLER, 2nd Lieut. J. C. G. ... 1912-17 *a*
Royal Engineers, 19th Corps Headquarters.

†VOWLER, Lieut. J. A. G. ... 1911-14 *a*
The Prince of Wales's Leinster Regiment (Royal Canadians), 3rd Bn. (Reserve), attached Machine Gun Corps; served in France; died of accidental wounds in Netley Hospital, July, 19th, 1917.

*WADE-GERY, Major H. T. ... 1913-14 *Master*
The Lancashire Fusiliers, 9th (S.) (3rd Salford) Bn.; M.C.

WAITHMAN, Rev. F. W. T. ... 1892-6 *a*
Chaplain to the Forces, 4th Class; in France and Mesopotamia.

WAITHMAN, Capt. J. C. ... ... 1888-93 *a*
The Queen's (Royal West Surrey) Regiment; Supernumerary Company, 2/5th Bn.

*WAKEFIELD, Major (a./Lieut-Col.) T. M. ... ... ... 1892-5 *a*
Royal Garrison Artillery; mentioned in despatches (twice); D.S.O.

†*WALKER, 2nd Lieut. E. B. ... 1902-7 *f*
The Queen's Own (Royal West Kent Regiment), 1st Bn.; mentioned in despatches; killed on Hill 60, near Ypres, April 18th, 1915.

WALKER, Lieut. R. D. ... ... 1911-14 *f*

The Dorsetshire Regiment, 6th (S.) Bn. (1914 to 1915); Royal Flying Corps (1915 to 1919).

*WALLER, Bt. Lieut.-Col. (temp. Brig.-Gen.) R. L. ... ... ... 1887-90 *a*

Royal Engineers, 86th Field Company, 21st Division; mentioned in despatches; C.M.G.

*WALSH, Col. H. A., C.B. ... 1868-71 *c*

Retired; Commanding No. 8 District.

†WALTER, 2nd Lieut. W. G. A. ... 1902-7 *a*

Australian Field Force, 48th Bn.; killed on the Somme, August 6th, 1916.

†WARD, 2nd Lieut. E. S. ... 1911-14 *g*

Gentleman Cadet, Royal Military College, Sandhurst; 3rd Bn., Oxfordshire and Buckinghamshire Light Infantry; attached to R.A.F.; missing, presumed killed, August 10th, 1917.

WARD, Capt. H. G. L. ... ... 1910-13 *a*

The Worcestershire Regiment, attached to 5th Bn. (Reserve); served in France with 2nd and 5th Bns., June, 1915, to June, 1918; then transferred to Indian Army, 2/102nd King Edward's Own Grenadiers; twice wounded.

WARING, 2nd Lieut. R. T. T. ... 1914-17 *g*

Royal Air Force; served in France as pilot with 54th Squadron.

†WARNER, Lieut. A. A. J. ... 1907-8 *c*

Singapore Defensive Force; and Grenadier Guards; killed in France, August 24th, 1918.

WARNER, Capt. C. T. ... ... 1904-7 *c*

22nd Punjabis, Double Company Officer; prisoner, after Siege of Kut-el-Amarah, from December 5th, 1915, to April 29th, 1916.

†WARNER, 2nd Lieut. C. W. ... 1914-16 *c*

Indian Army; 3rd Skinners Horse; died of pneumonia at Quetta, October 14th, 1918.

WARREN, Lieut. F. ... ... 1892-6 *f*

The King's Royal Rifle Corps, 4th Bn.; also served with 17th and 20th Bns.; twice wounded.

*WATERALL, Capt. H. G. ... 1899-1900 *b*

The Prince of Wales's (North Staffordshire Regiment), 1st Bn.; mentioned for War Services.

WATKINS, Corpl. J. R. ... ... 1909-11 *d*

4th Royal Irish Dragoon Guards and Machine Gun Corps Cavalry (1914 to 1919); served in France.

WATNEY, Capt. C. W. ... ... 1895-8 *a*

Indian Army.

*WATNEY, 2nd Lieut. R. G. ... 1910-12 *a*

R.N.R., H.M. Yacht Valiant; D.S.C.

*WATTS, Col. Sir W., K.C.B., C.B., V.D. ... ... ... 1872-4 *b*

The Welsh Regiment; Commanding 13th (S.) (2nd Rhondda) Bn., also 20th (Reserve) (3rd Rhondda) Bn.; and, during latter part of war, 1st City of London Cadet Brigade; mentioned in despatches.

*WATTS, 2nd Lieut. T. P. W. ... 1912-15 *g*
Royal Air Force; A.F.C.

WAUGH, 2nd Lieut. A. R. ... 1911-15 *a*
The Dorsetshire Regiment, attached to Machine Gun Corps; prisoner from March 28th to November 24th, 1918.

WAYMOUTH, Ridley ... ... 1911-14 *Prep.*
Royal Navy; 1917, H.M.S. Glorious; 1919, H.M. Destroyer Vanessa, acting in Baltic.

WEALLENS, Capt. W. R. W. ... 1910-14 *a*
2/4th Gurkha Rifles; served in Mesopotamia.

†WEBB, 2nd Lieut. G. T. ... 1905-7 *f*
Royal Fusiliers; killed in France, April 18th, 1916.

WEBB, Lieut. J. L. S. ... ... 1911-15 *b*
The South Wales Borderers; 4th Bn.; served in Mesopotamia; was on board Cameronian when torpedoed, April 15th, 1917.

WEBB, 2nd Lieut. M. H. ... 1909-12 *b*
The South Wales Borderers, 14th (S.) Bn.

WEBB, Lieut. W. E. K. ... 1909-12 *b*
O.C. 242nd Heavy Siege Battery Ammunition Column on the Somme, France; 1917, wounded; previously served with Caterpillar Tractor Depôt, Aldershot, and as O.C. Transport Experimental School of Gunnery, Shoeburyness.

WELD, Lieut.-Col. A. E. ... 1885-9 *b*
Royal Army Medical Corps.

WELLS, Pte. W. A. ... ... 1900-5 *b*
Canadian Expeditionary Force; 1st British Columbia Regiment.

WEST, 2nd Lieut. F. R. ... 1908-12 *a*
The King's Royal Rifle Corps, 15th (S.) Bn.

WESTALL, N. E. H. ... ... 1915-18 *f*
Entered Royal Air Force, Autumn, 1918.

WESTCOTT, 2nd Lieut. G. F. ... 1907-9 *a*
Royal Air Force.

WESTERN, Lieut. J. W. ... ... 1883-9 *a*
R.N.V.R.; Base Intelligence, Admiral's Office, Queenstown.

WESTLAKE, Cadet B. A. ... 1914-17 *b*
Cavalry Squadron; Inns of Court O.T.C.

WESTLAKE, Capt. M. E. K. ... 1910-14 *b*
The Northumberland Fusiliers, 7th (S.) Bn.; posted to Labour Corps, April, 1917, and served in France from that date.

†WHATELY, Lieut. P. V. V. ... 1911-15 *b*
179th Machine Gun Company, 60th Division; served in France, Salonika and Palestine; killed, December 27th, 1917, in the defence of Jerusalem.

WHATLEY, Lieut. L. S. ... ... 1895-7 *T.*
Royal Army Service Corps (M.T.).

WHEELER, 2nd Lieut. E. J. ... 1912-16 *f*
Royal Garrison Artillery, 1/1st Lancs. Heavy Battery, B.E.F.

WHEELER, Lieut. F. O. ... ... 1909-14 *b*

Royal Field Artillery, 2/4th East Anglian Ammunition Column (T.); served in Mesopotamia.

*WHINNEY, Major H. F. ... ... 1892-6 *f*

The Royal Fusiliers (City of London Regiment), 4th Bn.; mentioned in despatches; D.S.O.; O.B.E.

WHITAKER, 2nd Lieut. R. M. A. ... 1895-9 *b*

The Dorsetshire Regiment, 6th (S.) Bn.

*WHITE, Major R. K. ... ... 1895-7 *a*

Royal Army Medical Corps; mentioned in despatches (twice); D.S.O.

WHITE, Cadet W. S. R. ... ... 1914-16 *d*

Bristol University O.T.C.

WHITEHEAD, Lieut. A. ... ... 1901-4 *c*

Royal Army Service Corps.

*WHITEHEAD, Major B. ... ... 1903-5 *c*

Royal Army Medical Corps (Field Ambulance) and D.A.D.M.S. of the 29th Division, B.E.F., France; M.C.

WHITEHEAD, 2nd Lieut. G. M. ... 1901-2 *b*

Alexandra, Princess of Wales's Own Yorkshire Regiment, 8th (S.) Bn.

WHITELEY, Capt. G. T. ... ... 1887-92 *d*

The Cheshire Regiment, 6th Bn.; attached 23rd Bn.

*WHITFORD, Major C. E. ... 1884-7 *c*

The Duke of Cornwall's Light Infantry, 1/5th Bn. (T.); T.D.

WHITFORD, Cadet E. R. ... 1914-18 *c*
Membland Hall, Cadet Battalion.

†WHITFORD-HAWKEY, Lieut. A. H. 1913-17 *c*
Royal Flying Corps; killed in action in the air (North of Bapaume, over the German lines), on May 9th, 1918.

WHITING, Lieut. H. N. ... ... 1910-14 *a*
Prince Albert's (Somerset Light Infantry), 2/5th Bn. (T.); served in India.

†WHITNEY, 2nd Lieut. T. G. ... 1911-15 *a*
The Royal Warwickshire Regiment, 3rd Bn. (Reserve), attached 2nd Bn.; accidentally killed at Parkhurst, Isle of Wight, June 15th, 1916.

WHITTINGDALE, Lieut. J. ... 1908-13 *T.*
Royal Army Medical Corps; S.R.; served with British Red Cross, in Russia, 1915 to 1916.

WHITTINGDALE, T. Y. ... ... 1910-13 *T.*
Army Pay Corps; discharged, medically unfit, 1917.

†WHITTINGSTALL, 2nd Lieut. G.H.F. 1907-9 *a*
The Northumberland Fusiliers, 2nd Bn.; killed in action in France, August 3rd, 1916, when attached to 11th Bn.

WICKHAM, Cadet H. G. L. ... 1914-18 *a*
Inns of Court O.T.C. (Mounted Detachment).

†WICKINGS-SMITH, B. G. ... 1901-3 *c*
Drowned on the 'Lusitania,' May 7th, 1915.

Wight, Capt. A. J. L. ... ... 1907-12 *b*

The Hampshire Regiment, 2/9th (Cyclist) Bn. (T.).

*Wight, Lieut. C. H. ... ... 1910-15 *b*

The Middlesex Regiment, 18th Bn.; M.C.

†*Wildman, Capt. A. H. ... 1903-8 *b*

130th King George's Own Baluchis (Jacob's Rifles); with the I.E.F. in South Africa; mentioned in despatches; killed at Maktau, East Africa, September 14th, 1915.

Wildman, Paymaster-Lieut. T. B. 1902-7 *b*

Royal Naval Reserve; Vice-Consul at Puerto Moutt, Chile; served on H.M.S. Otranto.

*Wildy, Lieut. C. W. ... ... 1909 *a*

Inns of Court O.T.C., 1915; 2/5th Bn., London Regiment, December 25th, 1915; attached 10th Bn., Duke of Wellington's Regiment, July, 1917; seconded R.E. Signals, August, 1918; mentioned in despatches.

*Williams, Major-Gen. G., C.B. ... 1874-6 *a*

Late R.E.; Director General of Military Works, India; K.C.I.E.; mentioned in despatches.

*Williams, Bt. Lieut.-Col. (temp. Brig.-Gen.) G. C. ... ... 1895-8 *c*

Royal Engineers, 173rd (Tunnelling) Company; mentioned in despatches (7 times); Order of St. Stauislaus; C.M.G.; D.S.O.

Williams, Major N. J. ... 1897-1904 *T.*

Royal Army Service Corps.

WILLIAMS, Lieut. R. W. ... 1909-12 *a*

The East Surrey Regiment; 4th Bn.; served with 8th Bn., in France; July 1st, 1916, wounded; February, 1917, posted to 30th Training Reserve Bn., Brigade and Battalion Lewis Gun Officer; January, 1918, Battalion Lewis Gun Officer with 4th Bn., East Surrey Regiment, till discharged, December, 1918; then appointed Assistant Adjutant, No. 1 Dispersal Unit, Crystal Palace.

WILLIS, Major F. W. ... 1896-1900 *a*

Royal Garrison Artillery, 246 Siege Battery; served in France, 1914-15; in Mesopotamia, 1916 to 1918.

WILLOUGHBY, Capt. J. H. ... 1910-13 *d*

Royal Marine Light Infantry; formerly in 10th Bn., Royal Marine Brigade, Royal Naval Division.

WILLS, Hon. Capt. G. V. P. ... 1903-5 *d*

Royal Field Artillery, 1st South Midland Brigade, 2nd Gloucestershire Battery (T.) (Reserve).

WILSON, 2nd Lieut. E. A. R. ... 1897-1902 *a*

The London Regiment, 3/13th (Princess Louise's Kensington Regiment); previously a rifleman in 9th London Regiment (Queen Victoria's Rifles).

*WILSON, Rev. P. H. ... ... 1896-1901 *a*

Army Chaplain's Department; 22nd Wing, Royal Air Force, from November, 1916; previously, 1st Brigade, Scottish Horse; Military O.B.E.; mentioned in despatches.

†*Wilson, 2nd Lieut. R. A. ... 1905-9 *a*

The Durham Light Infantry; 4th Bn. (T.F.), attached 6th Bn.; killed at Estaires, April 9th, 1918; M.C.

Wilson, Capt. R. H. ... ... 1900-4 *a*

Indian Army; 82nd Punjabis; seconded for service with Frontier Militia; 2nd in Command, Kurram Militia.

Wilson, 2nd Lieut. R. M. ... 1905-9 *a*

Royal Engineers, Signalling Service; Motor Cycle Despatch Rider from September 7th, 1914, to January 26th, 1918.

*Winch, Lieut.-Col. A. B. ... 1897-1901 *f*

2nd Dragoons (Royal Scots Greys); Adjutant 1st Royal North Devon (Hussars) Yeomanry; O.B.E.

Winch, Major J. G. ... ... 1892-7 *f*

1/1st Royal East Kent (Duke of Connaught's Own) (Mounted Rifles) Yeomanry (T.F.); attached to Tank Corps; served in Gallipoli and Egypt; Commanded 3/1st Royal East Kent Yeomanry, August, 1916, to January, 1917; as Capt., Reserve Household Bn., at Windsor, January, 1917, to February, 1918.

Winch, Lieut. T. M. ... ... 1885-91 *f*

Royal Air Force.

*Windle, Lieut. B. G. ... ... 1912-16 *g*

Royal Air Force; served in France with 102nd Squadron; prisoner of war, 1917; repatriated, 1918; D.F.C.

†WINN-SAMPSON, 2nd Lieut. A. H. 1901-4 *d*
The Duke of Cambridge's Own (Middlesex Regiment), 5th Bn. (Reserve), attached 4th Bn.; killed, July 1st, 1916.

WOOD, Pte. A. D. ... ... 1895-9 *T.*
The Royal Fusiliers (City of London Regiment), 18th, 19th, 20th and 21st (S.) (1st, 2nd, 3rd and 4th Public Schools) Bns.; 'B' Coy., 2nd Bn.; invalided out, November, 1914.

WOOD, Pte. R. S. ... ... 1914-17 *d*
Artists Rifles, 2nd Bn., and No. 1 Infantry Officer, Cadet Bn., Near Plymouth.

†WOOD, 2nd Lieut. T. H. H. ... 1914 *Master*
The Dorsetshire Regiment, 3rd Bn. (Reserve), attached 1st Bn.; killed, near St. Eloi, April 13th, 1915.

WOODFORDE, Sergt. W. H. B. ... 1897-1901 *c*
Malay States Volunteer Rifles.

WOODHAMS, Lieut. J. P. ... 1897-1900 *d*
The Royal Sussex Regiment, 8th Bn.; wounded, April 9th, 1918.

WOODHAMS, Capt. R. E. ... 1899-1902 *d*
General List, attached to Lands Directorate, Headquarters, Eastern Command.

WOODHEAD, 2nd Lieut. F. C. T. ... 1914 *Master*
Unattached List (T.F.).

*WOODHOUSE, Capt. D. E. M. ... 1910-14 *a*
The Queen's Own (Royal West Kent Regiment), 7th (S.) Bn.; served in France; Instructor at 10th Officer Cadet Battalion from March, 1918; wounded four times; M.C.

WOODHOUSE, Lieut.-Col. F. D. ... 1878-81 *Price*
Dorsetshire Regiment, 4th Bn. (T.F.) (Reserve).

WOODHOUSE, Lieut. (a./Capt.) R. F. 1909-14 *a*
Royal Field Artillery, 3rd Wessex Brigade, 3rd Dorsetshire Battery (T.); served in India and Mesopotamia with 336th Brigade, R.F.A.

WOODS, 2nd Lieut. L. N. W. ... 1906-7 *a*
Canadian Expeditionary Force, Canadian Infantry and Light Horse, and Royal Naval Air Service.

*WOODWARD, Capt. W. H. 1877-1881 *Price*
Nyasaland Field Force; Military Landing Officer, Chinde, Portuguese East Africa; Administrative Commandant British forces at Chinde and acting Naval Transport Officer, July, 1917, to June, 1919; mentioned in despatches.

WREFORD, Lieut. V. S. J. ... 1913-14 *d*
Royal Field Artillery, 2/1st Northumbrian Brigade; served in Mesopotamia with the 102nd Brigade; invalided out.

*WRIGHT, Capt. C. W. G. ... 1903-5 *f*
Prince Albert's (Somerset Light Infantry); Staff Capt., Headquarters, No. 4 District; served in France; M.C.

*WRIGHTSON, Lieut. A. J. H. ... 1896-1900 *a*
Canadian Expeditionary Force; 1st British Columbia Regiment, 7th Bn.; M.C.

†WYATT-SMITH, Pte. H. H. ... 1912-15 *b*
28th (County of London) Bn. (Artists' Rifles); died of appendicitis, February 17th, 1916.

†WYATT-SMITH, 2nd Lieut. J. D. ... 1913-17 *b*

Royal Flying Corps; killed in Italy, on March 17th, 1918, owing to an accident to his machine when leaving aerodrome.

*WYLEY, Capt. D. F. H. ... ... 1901-2 *a*

Served in India, Mesopotamia and France; Staff Capt., 3rd Echelon, G.H.Q.; D.A.A.G. (Wimereux Record Section); metioned in despatches (thrice); O.B.E.; M.C.

†*WYLIE, Lieut. A. W. ... ... 1905-9 *f*

The Lincolnshire Regiment, 2nd Bn.; mentioned in despatches; killed at Neuve Chapelle, March 10th, 1915.

†*WYNNE, Lieut. M. O. M. ... 1906-8 *d*

Royal Field Artillery; mentioned in despatches; killed at Armentières, August 28th, 1915.

YATES, Lieut. R. A. ... ... 1913-17 *a*

Royal Air Force; prisoner of War at Rastall.

YEATMAN, Capt. G. D. ... ... 1902-4 *a*

The Dorsetshire Regiment, 2nd Bn.; attached Worcester Regiment.

YOUNG, Capt. F. H. McL. ... 1901-2 *T.*

The Gloucestershire Regiment, 1st Bn.

†*YOUNG, Capt. F. S. N. ... ... 1894-7 *c*

Royal Army Service Corps; mentioned in despatches; died in hospital at Bagdad, March 1st, 1918.

YOUNG, Lieut. G. A. ... ... 1910-14 *c*

The Duke of Edinburgh's (Wiltshire Regiment), 2/4th Bn. (T.); attached 39th Divisional Signal Company; 2nd Division N.W.F.F., India, and 68, Airline Section, E.E.F. (Palestine).

YOUNG, Capt. H. G. K. ... ... 1888-94 *a*

R.A.M.C.; served in France, 1916, to 1919, with 17th Division (53rd Field Ambulance and 7th Bn., The York and Lancaster Regiment) and 72nd General Hospital.

*YOUNG, 2nd Lieut. J. H. ... 1901-3 *T.*

Royal Army Service Corps (M.T.); mentioned in despatches (twice); D.S.O.; M.C.; Order of Redeemer.

YOUNG, L.-Corpl. R. K. ... ... 1902-6 *a*

Was rejected as medically unfit for British Army and enlisted, as a Private, in U.S.A. Army (Home Service).

# Roll of Honour.

Honeste Defunctorum
Memores Vivamus.

Abbott, Lieut. E. J. W.
Adamson, Capt. W.
Alderson, Capt. A. G. J.
Armstrong, Lieut.-Col. C. A.
Awdry, Lieut. W. W.

Bacchus, Capt. W. H. O.
Baker, Capt. C. D.
Baker, 2nd Lieut. G. L. J.
Bamford, Pte. A.
Barnes, Capt. J. E. T.
Barry, Capt. N. J. M.
Battersby, Capt. E. M.
Bawdon, 2nd Lieut. R. H.
Bayly, 2nd Lieut. V. T.
Bean, Lieut. C. R. C.
Beckton, Lieut. H.
Benbow, Pte. J. L.
Benison, 2nd Lieut. E. W.
Bennett, Sergt. B. C.
Bennett, Lieut. M. P.
Bennetts, Flt. Sub-Lieut. E. A.
Betts, Flt. Sub-Lieut. C. C.

Blair, 2nd Lieut. G. Y.
Blandford, Pte. C. E.
Blencowe, Capt. E. C. B.
Bligh, 2nd Lieut. E.
Bond, Capt. C. G.
Bowen, Lieut. E. G. A.
Brine, Lieut. E. L.
Broadrick, Major F. B. D.
Brooke, Capt. G. D.
Brown, Lieut. O.
Burgess, 2nd Lieut. P. G.

Campbell, 2nd Lieut. D. G.
Capel-Cure, Capt. B. A.
Card, 2nd Lieut. S. H.
Carr-Ellison, Capt. O. F. C.
Carrington, Capt. H. E.
Caruthers-Little, Capt. A.W. P.
Chatteris, Capt. T. B.
Chichester, Capt. R. G. I.
Clapton, 2nd Lieut. A.
Clark, Capt. H. C.
Clarke, Pte. W. W. E. M.
Clatworthy, 2nd Lieut. T. E.
Collot, 2nd Lieut. T. A.
Crawhall, Lieut. N. G.
Crichton, 2nd Lieut. A. G.
Croft-Smith, Lieut. E. S.
Crosby, 2nd Lieut. A. B. L.
Custance, Surg. G. W. M.

Dandridge, Lance-Corpl. A. P.
Dandridge, Lieut. W. L.
Duckworth, 2nd Lieut. W. H.
Duvall, Rev. (Capt.) J. R.

Eagar, Lieut. D. G.
Eagar, Lieut. F. R.

Edwards, Major B.
Egerton, 2nd Lieut. B. R.
Elliott, 2nd Lieut. E.
Elliott, 2nd Lieut. W. E.
Ellis, Major C. A.
Elsmie, Lieut.-Col. G. E. D.

Fenn, Lieut. E. J. P.
Findlay, Capt. R. de C.
Fitch, 2nd Lieut. D.
Foley, Pte. E. B.
Folliott, 2nd Lieut. J.
Forrest, Lieut. E. A. A.
Fraser, 2nd Lieut. V. A. D.
Freund, Corpl. E. W. T.
Frost, 2nd Lieut. A. C.
Frost, Lieut. J. J.

Gerrard, Capt. P. N.
Gibbons, 2nd Lieut. J.
Goldsmith, Lieut. H. M.
Graham-Montgomery, Capt. G. J. E.
Gray, 2nd Lieut. G. E. M.
Gray, Capt. H. M.
Grierson, Lieut. S. V.
Grove, 2nd Lieut. P. C.
Groves, Corpl. J. S.
Groves, Lance-Corpl. R. E.
Gunning, Lieut. J. W.
Gwyther, Corpl. P. H.

Halliday, 2nd Lieut. C. G. R.
Hampton, Rifleman W.
Hay, Capt. G. W.
Herbage, Pte. S. H. W.
Hicks, Col. R. F.
Hodges, 2nd Lieut. H. B.
Hodgson, Lieut. R. E.

Holmes, 2nd Lieut. B. R. G.
Hooper, 2nd Lieut. L. J.
Hoskins, 2nd Lieut. F. D.
Hyland, 2nd Lieut. H. B.

Jackson-Taylor, 2nd Lieut. J. C.
Janasz, 2nd Lieut. J. G. G.
Jeffreys, Lieut. W. S.
Jenkins, Lieut. R. B.
Jesson, Major R. W. F.

Kendle, Major R. H.
Kestell-Cornish, Capt. R. V.
Kidner, Corpl. F. E.
King, 2nd Lieut. E. W.
Kitson, 2nd Lieut. E. G. T.

Lacey, 2nd Lieut. E. S.
Large, Capt. H. E.
Larnder, Lieut. E. M.
Leeds, 2nd Lieut. J. S.
Legge, Capt. R. G.
Leigh, 2nd Lieut. H. G. T.
Limbery, Capt. C. R.
Limbery, Capt. K. T.
Llewellin, 2nd Lieut. W. M. J.
Lloyd, Lieut. G. L. B.
Lott, Lieut. J. C.
Luard, Lieut.-Col. E. B.

Macwhirter, Major T.
Mansel-Pleydell, Lieut. E. M.
Marsh, Capt. E. W. H.
Marson, 2nd Lieut. J. C.
Martin, 2nd Lieut. C.
Maunsell, Capt. R. G. F.
May, Lieut. H. G.
May, Lieut. T. R. A.
McEnery, Capt. J. A.

McGowan, 2nd Lieut. J. S.
Milligan, 2nd Lieut. A.
Montgomerie, Capt. W. G.
Moore, 2nd Lieut. R.
Moore, Tr. R. T.
Moritz, 2nd Lieut. O. F.
Murray, Major T. F.
Muspratt, Capt. K. K.
Muspratt, Capt. T. P.

Northey, Lieut. A.
Nutter, 2nd Lieut. G. H. E.

Ollivier, Major G. L.
Openshaw, Capt. G. O.

Palmer, Sub-Lieut. E. J.
Palmer, Lieut. L. S.
Parry, Lieut.-Col. C. F. P.
Parry-Jones, Capt. O. G.
Parsons, Capt. M. H. D.
Pearson, Cadet. C. R.
Penruddocke, Lieut. C.
Poore, Lieut.-Col. R. A.
Powell, Lieut. E. L.
Price, 2nd Lieut. E. W. M.
Prichard, Major R. G. M.

Puckridge, Capt. C. F. H.
Ramsay, Lieut. D. W.
Ransford, Capt. C. G.
Read, Lieut. A. B.
Reeves, 2nd Lieut. L.
Reid-Taylor, Capt. A. A. C.
Richards, 2nd Lieut. J. D. E.
Robertson, Lieut. W. M.
Robinson, 2nd Lieut. B. S.
Rose, 2nd Lieut. H. P.
Ross, 2nd Lieut. R. C.

Russell, 2nd Lieut. P. A.
Rutherford, Pte. H. G. G.

Sanders, Capt. A. E.
Sawyer, Capt. R. H.
Sayres, Lieut.-Col. A. W. F.
Scarbrough, Capt. R. J.
Scott-Holmes, Lieut. B.
Shaw, Lieut. W. E.
Shippard, Pte. C. N. W.
Simmons, Capt. F. W.
Simmons, Capt. P. E. M.
Slade, Major R. B.
Slater, Lieut T. A. F.
Smith, Capt. D. G.
Smith, 2nd Lieut. L. S.
Smith, Capt. V. N.
Smyth, Capt. W. H.
Spurway, Lieut. G. V.
Spurway, 2nd Lieut. R. P.
Stacke, Lieut. O. G. N.
Staley, Lieut. F. C.
Stevenson, Lieut. L. W. H.
Streatfeild, 2nd Lieut. T. B. M.
Stuart-French (Stuart), Maj. C.H.
Swabey, 2nd Lieut. A. M. C.
Sweet, Capt. L. H.
Symons, Pte. H. N.

Terry, Lieut. J. E.
Trask, Lieut. C. W. T.
Tucker, 2nd Lieut. A. R. L.
Tuke, 2nd Lieut. A. H. S.
Turrell, 2nd Lieut. H. G.

Vacher, 2nd Lieut. G. H.
van Goethem, Capt. H. E.
Vicary, Capt. G. D.

Vincent, Capt. W.
Vinter, 2nd Lieut. R. B. W.
Vizard, Capt. H. T.
Vowler, Major D. F. S.
Vowler, Lieut. J. A. G.

Walker, 2nd Lieut. E. B.
Walter, 2nd Lieut. W. G. A.
Warner, Lieut. A. A. J.
Warner, 2nd Lieut. C. W.
Webb, 2nd Lieut. G. T.
Whately, Lieut. P. V. V.
Whitford-Hawkey, Lieut. A. H.
Whitney, 2nd Lieut. T. G.
Whittingstall, Lieut. G. H. F.
Wickings-Smith, Mr. B. G.
Wildman, Capt. A. H.
Wilson, 2nd Lieut. R. A.
Winn-Sampson, 2nd Lieut. A. H.
Wood, 2nd Lieut. T. H. H.
Wyatt-Smith, Pte. H. H.
Wyatt-Smith, 2nd Lieut. J. D.
Wylie, Lieut. A. W.
Wynne, Lieut. M. O. M.

Young, Capt. F. S. N.

www.ingramcontent.com/pod-product-compliance
Ingram Content Group UK Ltd.
Pitfield, Milton Keynes, MK11 3LW, UK
UKHW040015200726
13854UKWH00001B/212